SEAHENGE

A Contemporary Chronicle

BARNWELL'S TIMESCAPE

First published by
Barnwell's Timescape Publishing
Barnwell's Printing Works
Penfold Street
Aylsham
Norfolk
NR11 6ET

© *Matthew Champion 2000*

ISBN 0 9531851 3 3

Produced and printed in England by
Barnwell's Print Ltd
Barnwell's Printing Works
Penfold Street
Aylsham
Norfolk
NR11 6ET

<u>*Front Cover*</u>
Seahenge, February 1999 by Wendy George.
This image is available as both a print and a postcard. For more details contact Wendy George, 24 Goose Green Road, Snettisham, Kings Lynn, Norfolk. PE31 7PW.

CONTENTS

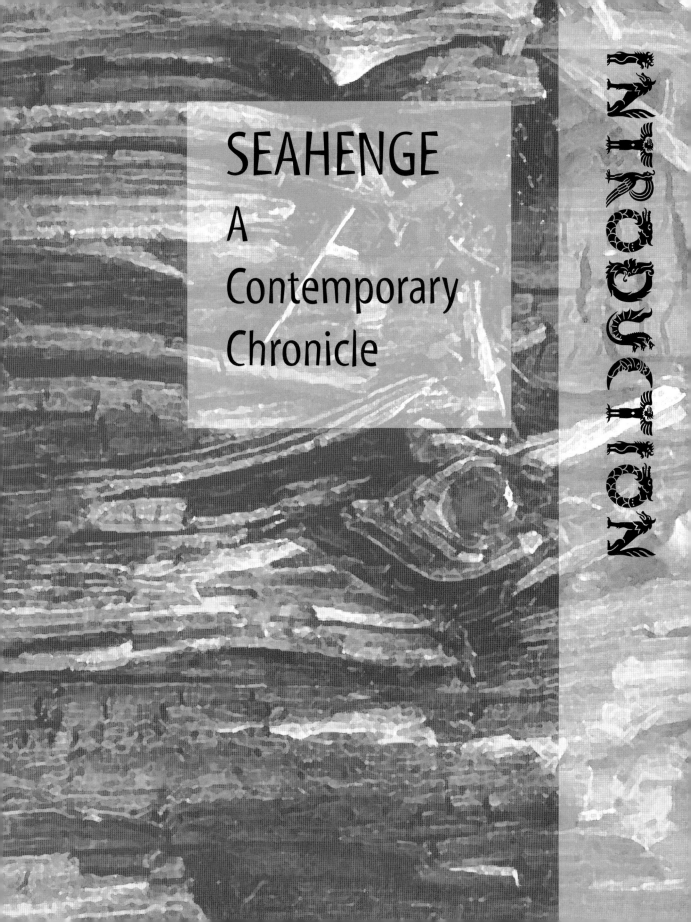

SEAHENGE

A

Contemporary

Chronicle

The Bronze Age timber circle discovered at Holme in North Norfolk, or Seahenge as it is more commonly known, was probably one of the most important archaeological discoveries to have occurred in Norfolk during the twentieth century; it was certainly one of the most controversial.

The re-appearance of a four-thousand-year-old timber monument among the bleak dunes of the windswept Norfolk coast in the early summer of 1998 led to one of the most hotly disputed and high profile archaeological excavations the county had ever known. For all those involved with the project, the archaeologists, the protesters and the local residents, nothing was ever going to be quite the same again. The monument, perhaps carrying with it some of its dark past, became the focus for protests and heated debates that influenced everyone who came into contact with it. No one who saw it, emerging from the waterlogged peat like the broken ribs of some long wrecked ship, could fail to be captured by its magic.

For some, searching for a sign at the end of the millennium, it was spiritual; a symbol of the beliefs and ideas of our long dead ancestors, for others it was purely historical; a glimpse into a distant era that we can only read about in history books. For everyone it held its own magic; a direct and tangible link with our past.

I first became aware of the discovery, like so many other local residents, from a report in the newspaper. There, splashed all over the front cover, was the dramatically told story of the re-emergence of the 'Stonehenge of the Sea'. The story itself said very little, for very little was then known about the site, but it was the photograph that caught my eye. The image used was a simple one. A dark circle of posts, barely poking their way out of the wet sand, and in the circle's centre a great dark mass that marked the roots and base of a massive oak tree. The picture contained no people; it simply disappeared and faded into a sea fringed horizon, and it was impossible to judge any scale. The circle could have been ten yards across or, just as easily, a hundred.

Long after the debate and arguments have faded it will be this image that I remember. As the weeks passed more information concerning the discovery began to emerge. At first it was little more than media speculation, the archaeologists having little they could confidently add to the debate, but even this was pounced upon by a henge-hungry public. Within weeks the monument was firmly placed in the public's mind as Stonehenge's little cousin by the sea, and by the time any real information came to light, released as and when it became available, a growing body of people had voiced their opposition to the site's excavation.

Ironically these early protesters were joined in their reluctance to see the circle lifted by no less a body than English Heritage. Believing that excavation and preservation would be a waste of valuable resources English Heritage stated that they wished only to record the monument before leaving it once more to the ravages of the North Sea. Eventually, under pressure from the British Council for Archaeology and the public, the powers that be at English Heritage changed their minds and proposed the excavation, removal and conservation of the circle.

By this time the fate of the timber circle was beginning to receive large amounts of media coverage. News hungry local journalists, perhaps sensing the debate and controversy that was to come, pounced on the story and began to milk it for all it was worth. Although no longer exclusively front page news the local papers were full of letters, editorial comment and follow up articles that picked up on every new development. The debate was on. No one who lived in the region could have been unaware of the circle's existence and everyone had their own opinion.

The highlight of the local media campaign appeared in the form of a four page 'Souvenir Pullout' issued by the Eastern Daily Press in January 1999. Across its back page the journalist had splashed the banner headline 'The big question is: should it be saved'? Now it really was the big question and one that is still largely open to debate even to this day. Both sides of the debate, those for excavation and those against, began to bring forth their arguments and present their cases to the public. However, amid all the name calling and heated argument sat two small, and rather beleaguered groups of people.

The first group, the local archaeologists, were beginning to attract the verbally hostile attention of the protesters and the media. For them it was a whole new experience: an experience they were entirely unprepared for. More normally used to standing on the same side as protesters they found the whole situation both difficult and stressful. The big guns had waded in on both sides and it was the local on the ground archaeologists who now found themselves on the front line.

If the site really was becoming a battle ground in the Seahenge debate then it was the local wildlife that began to suffer the first casualties. The circle was situated in the middle of an extremely sensitive nature reserve; a site so sensitive that its very existence was not even advertised. Suddenly this former out of the way stretch of coastline, a haven for bird life and rare breeding colonies, found itself the subject of national media attention. Despite calls from both the archaeologists and the Norfolk Wildlife Trust, the site's manager, for the public to stay away the numbers of visitors to the beach massively increased. Unable to resist the temptation members of the public 'just came for a quick look', with over 500 people arriving in one single weekend alone. The damage done to the surrounding wildlife was immense and still has to be fully assessed.

For anyone who had managed to avoid the debate surrounding the excavation it was finally brought, once again, to the nations attention by the screening of a *Time Team* programme devoted to the structure's discovery. This hour and a half programme, designed to show all sides to the story, perhaps raised even more questions than it answered. It polarised opinions and the debate, that had begun to die down, was once more thrown back into the limelight. Accusations of environmental vandalism and biased editing were freely bandied about and the damage done to the programme's reputation, until then almost spotless, has also still to be fully assessed.

In many respects the same can be said for the whole Seahenge debate; the full extent of the damage has yet to be assessed. All aspects of the discovery, excavation and reconstruction of the monument are still under close scrutiny by both the public and the protesters. Opinions have hardened, on both sides, and many lessons have been learnt. For everyone involved in the project things will never be the same again. Never again will archaeologists enter into such a project without first closely scrutinising the possible consequences. The media, they now realise, is a tool to be used; and if they don't utilise this, then someone else will. For the protesters similar lessons have presented themselves. It is not enough to simply make yourself heard if you shout too loudly then the public will go deaf to your pleas. If an argument is put forward then it has to be clear, well informed and concise. To do any less will do more harm than good.

At the end of the day, when Seahenge has receded into the distant past and become nothing more than a vague memory, it is these lessons that will be remembered. Archaeology in Norfolk, and perhaps nationally, has lost its innocence. There is, at least in the eyes of the media, no longer any black and white; only shades of grey, and everyone involved, the protesters included, walk the tightrope of public opinion. However, it must not be forgotten that many good things came out of the Seahenge project. We have learnt a great deal, both about ourselves and our attitudes to the past, as well as those people, our ancestors, who in the spring of 2050 BC took a bronze axe to a great oak tree.

It would have been impossible to have put together this publication without the kind and considerate help of a great number of people and organisations and to all those I express my sincere thanks. It would be impossible to mention them all by name but amongst these many dozens of helpful individuals I feel I must mention the special help and encouragement that I received from John Lorimer, who seems unable to walk a beach anywhere without finding something, and his wife Jackie, who has tirelessly put up with our constant phone calls. I would also like to thank Geoff Needham, the Chairman of Holme Parish Council, for taking time out of his busy schedule to talk with me on many occasions, and Rollo Maughfling, Archdruid of Britain for his advice and splendid narrative. I must also express my sincere thanks to Cath Saunt of BBC Radio Norfolk for her insights into all the media aspects of the story, the staff of Eastern Counties Newspapers Limited for allowing me to go through their photographic archive and Pat Fisher (www,northcoastal.freeserve.co.uk), who herself spent many hours recording the events on Holme beach. Finally, I would like to say a very special 'thank you' to my wife Rebecca for her interest and advice, and without whom none of this would have been possible.

In
the
beginning ...

CHAPTER 1

The village of Holme, or Holme-next-the-sea to give it its full and proper title, stands precariously on the coastline on the very north western tip of Norfolk. A bare couple of miles westwards around the coast, atop the red and white sandwiched layers of chalk and carrstone cliffs, lies the great Victorian seaside town of Hunstanton where penny arcades and ice cream parlours still jostle for space with high tech entertainments and sea-life centres. In the summer tourists throng the promenade, the beaches resound to the shrill cries of paddling children and the caravans form great wagon trains of white fibreglass as they wind their way along the inadequate Norfolk highways. And yet, amid the hustle bustle and noise of modern tourism Holme has somehow managed to remain apart; an isolated village of relative calm and tranquillity.

This is not to say that Holme is a backwater; a village entirely populated by Norfolk people who can trace their ancestors back to the time of Henry VIII. Far from it. Holme, like all other villages on the picturesque North Norfolk coast, has its share of 'incomers', summer visitors who never got round to leaving and people who have retired to the area in search of the peace and tranquillity of a country life. Yet it has retained its essential character. It is still a living, breathing community that, whilst welcoming the numerous visitors that migrate there during the summer months, does not close its doors and put up the shutters when the nights draw in.

Many of the locals quite happily believe that it is during the winter time that the area is at its most scenic. The coastline, fringed by the salt marshes and marron grass topped dunes so beloved of artists and film makers, is at its best during the winter time. With a sharp wind blowing in off the grey North Sea, the washed out and bleached sky and mile after mile of empty sand stretching away into the distance it is difficult not to find a bleak grandeur in the surroundings. It is, they say, a place of boundaries. Where the sea meets the shore and the sky meets the sea, and when you stand on a cold winter morning watching the rain squalls race across the blue grey water it is easy to believe that there is something special about the whole place; something almost spiritual.

However, you would not be the first person to find it so. Generations upon generations of local people have always known that there really was something special about this particular isolated corner of the county. They do not need to be told such things; they live amongst its splendour and hear its voice in the shrill cries of the gulls that wheel hungrily above the sand dunes.

Historians and archaeologists too concede that this area has always had a strong hold on the hearts and minds of the East Anglian people. As far back as recorded history can take us this small corner of Norfolk has been deeply significant and its importance is, as yet, hardly understood. The Iceni tribe, who under their queen Boudicca led a bloody revolt against Roman oppression, occupied this area and built a series of small hill-forts amid its shallow river valleys. Here too they worshipped their gods, burying great neck rings, or torcs, of gold and silver as a sacrifice to the deities.

These torcs, superbly made and a wonder of Celtic craftsmanship, appear to have been more than just an outward display of wealth. The image of these great golden neck rings appears on both contemporary sculptures and engravings and is assumed to have been a very potent symbol to the Celtic warrior. Polybius, the Greek historian, writing in the 3rd century BC describes the Celtic warriors he came across as 'very terrifying' and 'the naked warriors in front, all in the prime of life and finely built men, and all in the leading companies richly adorned with gold torcs and armlets'. And yet, it is to north west Norfolk we must look for perhaps the finest discovery of such sacrificed items. At Snettisham, a few miles around the coast from Holme, a great horde of such torcs was discovered. Buried at least several decades prior to the Roman invasion the true meaning of the sacrifice has yet to be understood.

However, with the Iceni gone, this area of Norfolk remained a centre of ceremony and belief, as well as remaining tactically important. The Romans themselves constructed one of the earliest, and most important, of the 'Saxon shore' forts at Brancaster, a few miles from Holme, and Little Walsingham, the great medieval pilgrimage centre, is now believed to have actually been built on the site of a Roman settlement and shrine complex. Further than this the 'Peddars Way', a Roman road constructed, it is believed, upon a much more ancient trackway and a feature that still influences the landscape to this day, actually ends at the village of Holme itself. At Hunstanton legend tells us that Saint Edmund, the last Anglo-Saxon King of East Anglia, landed to take up his throne while a little further south, at Bawsey,

Saxon monks established a small monastery overlooking the sea.

The village of Holme itself, like so many other Norfolk villages, has a deep rooted history. Standing squarely at the northern end of the Peddars Way it has always had something of a mysterious air. Those who have walked the ancient trackway that leads north from Thetford and find themselves eventually at Holme are sometimes puzzled. Despite the village's pleasant atmosphere and fine historic church there seems little reason for it to be marked in such a dramatic fashion. A road that leads, as it were, nowhere. Yet the Peddars Way has been there for well over two thousand years and points to an important past that even the local residents have now all but forgotten.

However, as much as the historians, archaeologists and local people actually realised the importance of this area in our history, in the early summer of 1998

few, if any of them, were prepared for what was about to happen. Nature was about to reveal to them all a long forgotten episode in the areas past and a new chapter was about to be written in the countie's history.

A Stray Find?

In the early spring of 1998 John Lorimer, a local child care and youth worker, was walking along the beach at Holme Dunes in the company of his brother-in-law Gary Wright. Both men knew the area well, having lived nearby for many years, and had often walked along the coast from Hunstanton. John was keen to investigate the nature reserve as a possible place to bring the children in his care on future visits. However, that morning both men had other matters on their mind.

Gary had just finished making a shrimp net for John and both men were keen to test it. Leaving their car in the nature reserve car park they walked down to the beach through the early spring sunshine. As they reached the foreshore they both realised that they had arrived a little early in the day; the tide was going out but shrimping was impossible until the water had reached the low water mark. Not wishing to just sit about and wait for the waters to recede John and Gary decided to make the best of their time at Holme and try their hand at a little crabbing amongst the peat scarps on the beach. Putting the new shrimping net aside for the time being both men began to search for the elusive edible crabs that were well known to frequent the area.

Crabbing, unfortunately, is not as easy as it sounds. The crabs themselves are less than keen on the activity and try to make life difficult for their adversaries by hiding themselves in the most out of the way places that they can find. Their favoured spots are hidden deep beneath any object that will afford them some protection and any potential crab fisherman must be prepared to search every hiding place; anywhere that the crab may take refuge. The two men split up as they wandered along the beach and peat scarp searching for the crabs. John Lorimer made his way across the foreshore keeping a sharp look out for likely hiding places. Then, sticking out of the peat, John noticed what appeared to be a large inverted tree trunk.

The trunk itself was standing just proud of the peat, with the horns of the tree roots standing only six or seven inches above the surface. John naturally assumed that the tree stump had been washed up onto the beach before settling itself into the soft peat and, realising that the tree roots would be a perfect hiding place for crabs, he began to search under the projecting roots. The task proved a fruitless one, John only just managing to get his fingers under the roots, and he soon abandoned the tree stump in favour of more promising sites.

Moving further out along the beach John began to search the area to the seaward side of the tree stump. Here, where the wave action was greater, the overlying peat had been washed off the clay layer upon which it rested and the boundary between the two provided perfect cover for the crabs. Eyes fixed firmly on the ground John walked slowly along the foreshore. Then, about twenty five feet to the seaward side of the tree stump, John came across an object simply lying on the surface of the clay. 'I called Gary over', writes John, 'and showed it to him. I guessed it might be a Bronze Age axe head'. Gary, however, was less impressed and suggested that it was nothing more

than a piece of scrap that had been washed up from the wreck of the 'Vicuna'.

The 'Vicuna' was still clearly visible from where John and Gary were standing on the beach. She had been carrying a cargo of ice, in the days before refrigeration technology, from Norway to Kings Lynn. Unfortunately, she had been caught in a heavy storm while approaching the English coast and had been forced to take refuge in Hull. However, the storm was too much for the ship and weighed down with her heavy cargo she had broken her moorings and been driven south by the gale. On the 7 March 1883 she had finally come to grief somewhere near Brancaster on the North Norfolk coast. Since then, due to the variable tides and frequent storms that batter the Norfolk coastline, she had been moved several times, finally coming to rest at Holme after a tidal surge in 1985; just over a century after she first went down.

John Lorimer, not entirely convinced by his brother- in-laws argument, put the metal object in his back pocket with the intention of studying it closer later on. The excitement over, both men returned to their search for crabs; in which they were not entirely unsuccessful. As the day progressed, and the tide finally went out to its fullest extent, John and Gary finally got a chance to try the new shrimp net. After several hours, and well pleased with the new net, the chill breeze finally got the better of them. 'When it became too cold', writes John, 'we decided to call it a day and walked back up the beach where two women were walking and playing with children. We cleaned the crabs and showed the children. This is when I had a good look at my find. I wiped it clean and showed it to them – it had a green patina and rust spots'.

The more John looked at his find the more he was convinced that is had not come from the 'Vicuna'. There was something about it that still made him cling to the belief that it was something more than scrap from a nineteenth century ship wreck. His original idea, that it was a Bronze Age axe head, may have seemed a little fanciful to Gary but John was intrigued and decided to take it home with him and carry out a little research of his own. 'On the way back to the car', writes John, 'I reported my find to one of the wardens at the Nature Reserve's shop so that they knew what I had found and told them I would be contacting the relevant authorities'.

When John returned home that afternoon he decided that, rather than contacting the museum immediately and risk wasting their time with a piece of nineteenth century scrap, he would try and discover what he had actually found. Over the next few weeks John, encouraged by his wife Jackie, began to investigate his mysterious find from Holme beach. Happily, luck was on his side and during a trip to the dentist in the following weeks John came across a metal detecting magazine in the dentist's waiting room. The magazine was full of pictures of recent treasure hunting discoveries and, much to his satisfaction, John found a picture of an object that was very similar to his find from the beach. The photograph's caption described the object as a Bronze Age axe head, just as he had first suspected, however, upon closer scrutiny John noticed that the object in the picture, while generally similar to his find, did show some very marked differences. The object that John had discovered was less flanged than that shown in the magazine. Nevertheless, convinced he was on the right track, John decided to take his research a step further.

His next port of call was the Norfolk Studies section of the reference library in Norwich. Here, among the many hundreds of volumes dedicated to Norfolk Archaeology, John began to discover that his find on Holme beach was not the first artefact of historical interest to have been found in the immediate area. According to the available records the beach had once been the scene for several intriguing discoveries. In the early 1900s a number of large tree stumps had been washed up in the area with what appeared to have been stone axe heads embedded in them. Although little further investigation had been done at the time, on the ground archaeology still being in its infancy, they had aroused considerable interest among the local archaeological community.

However, further research led John to discover that since the appearance of the tree trunks nearly a century before no further notable finds had been reported from the beach or foreshore. Continuing his delving into the local archives he further found that there appeared to be very little actually known about the Bronze Age history of the area around Holme Dunes. By now convinced that what he had in fact discovered was a Bronze Age axe, other pictures having come to light in the library, he realised that the discovery may well have been important and determined to contact the main county museum at Norwich Castle.

Now realising that he had more than just a piece of scrap metal John began to wonder what the situation would be regarding ownership of the artefact and what exactly his legal position would be if the find proved to be important. Determined to find answers to all his questions John phoned the museum. After giving a short description of the axe, and explaining the circumstances in which it was found, the museum asked if John would bring it in to them for evaluation and investigation. Pleased by the enthusiastic response John travelled to Norwich and, on the 20 July 1998, delivered his find into the hands of the museum staff.

The museum curators were quick to respond to John Lorimer's enquiry and had no trouble identifying his find from the beach. In a report sent to John in the following month they stated that the axe head was, without doubt, from the Bronze Age. Further to that, they also stated that another very similar axe (identified as a Group 1 primary pattern palstave) had been discovered on the beach at about the same time and had also been brought along to them for identification. However, John's axe could not be quite so easily identified. 'Because of its worn condition', the report went on, 'the date and type of this axe is not totally certain. Its outline and size suggests that it is probably an Irish palstave of group B, although it lacks certain features such as a mid rib and casting flash. Whether this is because of the sea erosion is impossible to tell. If it is an Irish group B', the report concluded, 'then it dates from the Action Park Phase, Circa 1600 – 1400 BC'

John Lorimer was delighted with the museum's report; he really had discovered a Bronze Age axe head. However, not all the news was good. On the return of the axe head John was informed by the museum staff that the axe itself was showing signs of 'bronze disease'. This disease, commonly known as bronze rot, is actually a chemical reaction taking place in the metal itself and was perhaps brought on by the sudden change in environment that the axe had undergone. The reaction, once started, can be so severe that, without suitable treatment in a specialist laboratory, eventually the whole object would disintegrate.

Having spent so long investigating his discovery the last thing John wanted was for it to simply rot away. Luckily, later events were to lead to an offer to conserve the axe from English Heritage and, unable to fund such an expensive procedure himself, John Lorimer jumped at the chance. The axe head was once

more taken away and is now undergoing specialist treatment by an expert at the Museum of London. However, before John once again relinquished his prize find, and unsure of when it would be returned, he decided to create a replica of the axe. With the help of a friend, who had some experience in bronze casting, John created a mould from the original axe. Then, melting down two brass taps and a ball-cock to supply the new metal, a perfect replica of the axe was cast. With his reproduction axe safely in his keeping John Lorimer sent the original off with English Heritage to be conserved.

Runners Ring

Meanwhile, whilst all the research and identification of the axe had been going on, John had returned to the beach at Holme Dunes on several occasions. His research had led him to conclude that Bronze Age artefacts were discovered, as often as not, in small hordes. Knowing that at least one other similar axe had been found on the beach (it later transpired that there was a third axe picked up at about this time) John hoped that he might be lucky enough to come across other artefacts from the period. However, during his subsequent visits to the area it was something else entirely that began to attract his attention.

It was nearing midsummer by this time and as the days had grown longer and the weather warmer John's visits to the beach at Holme had become more frequent. 'On one visit', writes John, 'I noticed three posts sticking out of the peat near the central upturned stump under which I had been previously crabbing with my family and friends'. It was this tree stump, first noticed by John back in the spring, that now began to attract his regular attention. On his subsequent visits over the next few weeks he began to notice that more and more posts were becoming visible as the peat was eroded by the constant actions of the sea. Most intriguing of all, John soon began to realise that the newly exposed posts were showing signs of being laid out in a rough circle and the large tree trunk, which John had originally thought had been washed up by the tide, was not only totally upright but also positioned directly in the circle's centre.

The circle was positioned midway between the low tide and high tide marks and was only visible for a few hours each day. Even then the timbers were never completely out of the water and the peat in which they were embedded always remained in a pool of water. Gradually, as the weeks passed, the rest of the upright posts began to emerge through the peat until at last a complete circle was clearly visible at low tide. The great tree stump, as John had begun to suspect, was clearly situated in the circle's centre. This realisation confirmed to John that the stump was not simply an additional piece of driftwood but was rather

The Salt Marshes of North West Norfolk. A constantly threatened enviroment and wildlife habitat. copyright - R. Treherne.

a deliberately placed and integral part of the circle itself. As John himself wrote, 'if it had been washed in it would have been to one side or at the edge of the circle and not central'.

The circle began to fascinate John. He kept up his visits to the site and became more and more convinced that the timber circle was in some way significant. In his quest to find out more about the feature John asked around locally, visiting the local pub, to try and discover if any of the residents knew anything about it. After all, this area of coastline had long been used for fishing and salt extraction, and the circle may have been nothing more than a relatively recent addition to the beach. However, none of the local people that John talked to could enlighten him and there seemed, at the time, little interest in his discovery. Undeterred John continued his quest for information.

In fact, in John Lorimer's immediate circle of friends and family the circle on Holme beach was becoming something of a standing joke. John, who's nick name locally is 'Runner', was convinced that he had discovered something important but those who knew him simply referred to it as 'Runners Ring'. Even John's

wife, Jackie, was becoming a little tired of the whole subject. Finally, she told him, that if he really believed the circle was important he should talk to the museum again. They had been extremely helpful with the axe head, even suggesting further books that John might find of interest, and if the circle was really significant they would be the ones to tell him. Spurred on by Jackie's advice John, once more, phoned Norwich Castle Museum.

The staff at the museum were, once again, very interested in John's discovery of the circle but were unable to shed any light upon the matter themselves. Instead, they suggested, John should contact the Norfolk Landscape Archaeological Unit situated at the Gressenhall Rural Life Museum. Following their advice John contacted the unit and was put through to Edwin Rose, the Sites and Monuments Record Officer. After a brief explanation of what John had found on the beach it was agreed that the two men should actually meet at the site.

The first visit by the archaeologist to the site was something of a disappointment for John Lorimer. He met Edwin Rose at the nature reserve and, because of the difficulty in actually locating the circle, he had to act as a guide. They had timed the visit well and most of the timbers were showing through the peat and seawater making it possible for Edwin Rose to take several photographs and make some rough measurements of the circle. In fact, as it turned out the structure was not a circle at all, but rather an ellipse that measured approximately 18 feet by 15 feet. As to what the structure was, and how old it might have been, Edwin Rose was unwilling to commit himself. However, Edwin Rose was pleased with the visit, being able to use the opportunity to investigate the elusive wreck of the 'Vicuna' that lay not far from the timber circle. The two men separated, Edwin Rose promising to write to John with any findings, and while John made his way back to the car park the archaeologist wandered off to investigate the ship wreck.

However, John initial disappointment at the archaeologist's reaction to his find was soon dispelled with the arrival on his doormat, several weeks later, of a letter from the Norfolk Archaeological Unit. The letter, signed by David Gurney, the units Principal Landscape Archaeologist, stated that 'the timber structure has created great excitement among my colleagues and we are trying to arrange funding for radiocarbon dating, proper planning and so on'. It

appeared that John's instinct that the circle was in some way important was based upon a firm foundation. The circle, and the axe that had led him to it, appeared to have been worth all the time he had spent on them. 'I was very excited', writes John, 'that the two finds could be connected in some way'. Runner's Ring was now more than just a family joke.

The letter from the Archaeological Unit was followed, later in the year, by a phone call. Bill Boismier and Mark Brennand, field archaeologists from the unit, wanted to make a personal visit to the site and assess the best course of action to be taken. Would John meet them at the nature reserve and guide them to the structure as they had been unable to locate it on a previous visit. John readily agreed and a few days later met the archaeologists at Holme and led them out to where the timbers were just becoming visible through the water. This time John was not disappointed; after studying the circle for a few minutes Bill Boismier turned around and said 'This is the real thing – this is ancient'.

'Bill Boismier's words', writes John Lorimer, 'thrilled me that I may have found something of significance and my excitement and curiosity grew as further information came to light'. Following the visit by Mark Brennand and Bill Boismier to the site, John was in regular contact with Bill Boismier at the archaeological unit and his superior, the then Principal Field Archaeologist, Brian Ayers. The unit knew that the site was important and that it was ancient but really knew very little else. Its exact age and usage were still a mystery and the only way that any light would be shed upon the matter was by further, on site, investigation. However, there was a catch.

The actual financial costs involved in even a simple preliminary investigation, site recording exercise and scientific dating of the monument would be extremely high and the Norfolk Archaeological Unit, already stretched for resources and on a tight budget, could not afford to undertake the exercise without some outside financial assistance. However, in certain cases, when the potential importance of a site appears to justify such action, the county archaeological units can apply to English Heritage for funding. Accordingly Bill Boismier drew up an initial project summary for the monument, including a proposal for action to be taken, and submitted it to English Heritage.

This project summary indicates that the Norfolk Archaeological Unit already suspected the true date of the structure at Holme as it states that 'wooden structures of the Bronze Age and prehistoric date in general are exceedingly rare and in need of further investigation'. The report goes on to list the aims of the proposed project as follows:-

● To determine the extent, condition, nature, quality and date of the structure.

● To provide a record of the structure and a characterisation of the wood working technology involved in its construction.

● To establish, as far as possible, the sequence of any modifications or repairs to the structure.

● To obtain wood samples for radiocarbon dating and examples of the wood working technology employed in its construction.

● To recover any associated artefactual and ecofactual materials associated with the site which may assist in its interpretation.

● To disseminate the archaeological data obtained from the project in a manner appropriate to that data.

The report put together by Bill Boismier was well received at English Heritage and £9000 was made available to the unit to carry out the initial research, radiocarbon dating and trial excavation at the site. Geoffrey Wainwright, then Chief Archaeologist at English Heritage, was keen to discover more about the monument and gave the project his full approval. A report, put together by the archaeologists at the end of the initial assessment, would recommend what course of action, if any, was needed in the future.

Trial Excavation

The assessment began in the November of 1998 and involved a full site survey, including the locating of the monument within the Ordnance Survey grid using a global positioning system, and a small trial excavation. The Global Positioning System, or GPS as it is commonly known, is one of the most advance mapping systems currently available. It relies on a system of twenty four satellites that orbit the earth at a height of over 10,000 miles every twelve hours. These satellites each emit a continuous navigation signal which is picked up by a hand held receiver on the ground. By comparing the signals of three or more satellites, circling the earth in known orbits, it is possible for the receiver to calculate its exact position to within less than 100 metres. An updated system, currently only available to the military, can plot an even more precise position on the earth's surface; reputedly to within three metres. Using this system the archaeologists were easily able to accurately plot Seahenge on the map.

The excavation itself immediately produced some intriguing and fascinating results that even some of the archaeologists were surprised at. The central tree trunk was examined in detail and it became obvious that some of the markings upon its surface were, in fact, man made. The marks themselves were subsequently identified as having been made by a bronze axe; an axe very similar to that which John Lorimer had found nearby. The fact that the tool marks were still clearly visible amazed many of those involved with the trial excavation. Such evidence has normally been destroyed by the passing of the centuries and the timber circle provided the first opportunity to study such tool marks from a complete Bronze Age site in Britain.

It was further established that the circle, far from originally being built on the beach, was actually constructed in an area of salt marsh that was originally between one and three miles from the coastline (depending on which report you believe). This salt marsh would have been the area behind the sand dunes, criss crossed with small rivers and streams, and it was even possible that the circle stood on a small island within the marsh. Over the centuries the sea has eaten into the coastline, exposed the marsh and peat beds that it had laid down, and eventually

brought the circle to light. Environmental and pollen samples were also extracted from the surrounding peat and should, once analysis has taken place, give a clear picture of the surrounding vegetation at the time of the circle's construction.

A small excavation working down one side of the tree trunk also revealed a fibrous rope-like material that appeared to be contemporary with the trunk. This material was later identified as being thick strands of honeysuckle and the plant stems had obviously been used as a rope during the trunk's original positioning: the only find of this type ever to have turned up in Britain. The archaeologists also took the opportunity to examine the outside circle of finger posts in some detail. To provide a sample for radiocarbon dating, as well as establishing exactly how far the timbers were actually embedded in the beach, one of the finger posts was excavated and lifted. It transpired that the finger posts extended a little over a metre below the surface and went clean through the surface peat to the clay layer beneath.

The external finger post was then removed from the site for preservation and radiocarbon dating (leading to several confusing reports as to how many posts actually made up the monument). The dating of the timbers was to be carried out by Alex Bayliss of Sheffield University, Scientific Dating Co-ordinator for English Heritage, in collaboration with colleagues from Queen's University, Belfast. However, as well as trying to establish a date for the outer finger posts it was decided that, as part of the project, an attempt should be made to date the central stump. After all, it was quite possible that the stump could pre-date the circle or visa versa, and Bill Boismier's original proposal to English Heritage clearly stated that they should 'establish, as far as possible, the sequence of any modifications or repairs to the structure'. To fail to date the central stump would be a gross oversight.

What happened next, and more importantly why it was allowed to happen, remains a little unclear. Several different versions of events have been circulated, some of which flatly contradict each other, and none of those directly involved are willing to talk on the record. Other archaeologists, none of whom it must be said were actually involved with the site, have expressed amazement at what was allowed to take place and all have agreed that it was a badly handled mistake. However, to understand the full extent of the tragedy it is first essential that you understand the methods used for dating ancient timbers.

One of the key elements in dating ancient timbers is a technique known as 'Dendrochronology', or simply tree ring dating. This method relies on taking a sample of the wood and matching the varying widths of the seasonal growth rings in the timber with a master record that goes back many thousands of years. This master record is only available for certain species of tree located in specific climate regions. Luckily the data available for oaks in northern Europe is quite extensive. However, it is not possible to use this technique on just any old piece of timber as the method relies upon having a sufficiently large number of visible tree rings to act as a comparison: forty to fifty rings usually being considered the required minimum.

In normal circumstances the sample taken from the timber is in the form of a drilled core, taken at right angles to the tree rings. This core sample should include as many tree rings as possible, including the heartwood, and can vary in size up to about an inch and a half. However, for some reason, when it came to extracting a core sample from the central tree stump of the Holme circle this method was not used. Various stories have been circulated, some claiming that the timber was too soft to allow a proper core sample, others that it was too hard, but whatever the truth of the matter the archaeologists decided to use a different method altogether. Instead a chainsaw was used to cut into the central stump and extract a large 'V' shaped slice from the timber. This massive wedge shaped slice cut right down into the heart of the stump, reaching the very core of the tree, and causing irreparable damage.

The damage caused by the extraction of the dating timbers has since become a focus for debate and has been picked up on by many of the protesters who later became involved with the project. English Heritage and the Norfolk Archaeological Unit state that the site archaeologists were unhappy about treating the timbers in such a manner and only did so on the advice of the dating specialists. These 'specialists', unfortunately, were not on site and did not understand the true situation surrounding the discovery. Had they been so it is unlikely that they would have proposed such a radical sampling technique. If they had anticipated the full excavation and removal of the timber circle they would have suggested a much less damaging, and visible, approach. However, the real reason for their actions is unlikely to have been either malicious or simple incompetence. The true reasons behind their approach is likely to have been those suggested by John Lorimer. 'The reason they chain sawed such a large, and since, controversial piece from the central stump', writes John, 'was that they were originally going to leave it (the circle) to the sea. They had not even thought about lifting it'.

David Miles, who was later to take over from Geoffrey Wainwright as Chief Archaeologist at English Heritage, has since been reported as saying, upon several separate occasions, that the use of the chainsaw on the circle timbers was a mistake. At a meeting held later between all sides in the debate he is reported to have said that he was 'profoundly sorry that a chainsaw had been used'. However, none of those involved in the incident are willing to talk about it 'on the record' and it remains likely that no official explanation will be forthcoming.

With the timber samples taken and the initial recording and trial excavations complete the archaeologists left the site to draw up their reports. The results from the dating process were not going to be available for many months but, in the mean time all those experts who had been involved in the recording exercise went away to mull over the few facts that they now had available to them and draw up the series of recommendations that would be passed on to English Heritage. These recommendations, although stressing the unique aspects of the circle, did not wholeheartedly back the idea of large scale excavation and preservation of the monument, rather stressing the need for further investigation and thorough recording.

In response to the report from the site archaeologists, and bearing in mind the complexity and expense of a full scale rescue excavation, English Heritage took the view that the circle should now be left to the ravages of the sea. The site should be monitored on a regular basis but no further large scale action was planned. However, just when the archaeologists thought that they had done with the circle at Holme Dunes the story took another twist. The media got hold of the story and suddenly everything that had seemed so certain a few weeks earlier was now up in the air again; the sand had shifted beneath their feet.

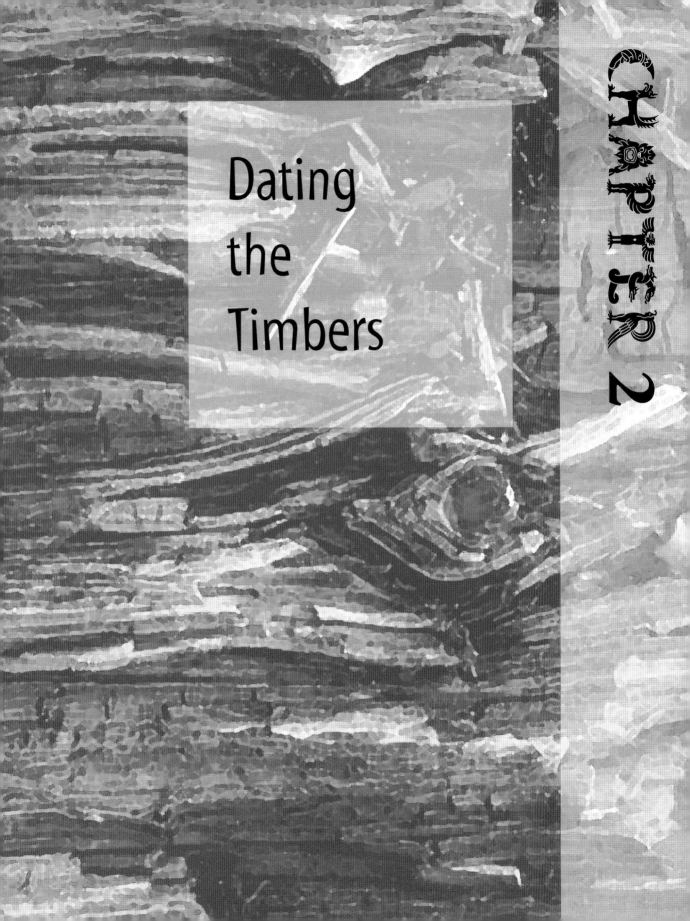

Dating the Timbers

One of the most fascinating, and exciting, stories surrounding of the whole Seahenge saga is that of the dating of the actual timbers themselves. From visual and associated evidence, that of the axe found by John Lorimer and the axe made wood working marks on the timbers, the archaeologists had a fairly clear idea that the circle dated to the Bronze Age but beyond that they could not really go. However, the Bronze Age is a massive period in time, stretching from around 2250 BC to about 500 BC, and it was essential that the archaeologists narrowed this time-scale down. Even allowing for the fact that the axe that John Lorimer discovered came from around 1500 BC their was no way of being sure that this date corresponded to the time when the circle was first built. The archaeologists needed a more precise and scientific method of dating the circle.

The methods employed by the scientists working for English Heritage were complex and involved using two established dating techniques combined with a method of statistical analysis invented over two centuries previously, but only recently re-introduced.

In fact, this was the first major archaeological discovery on which this new combination of techniques had been used, and the results were, to say the least, startlingly accurate. Rather than just giving the archaeologists a general date, usually prefixed with a variable of plus or minus a certain number of years, the scientists were able to provide an exact date for the circle's construction. As if this was not exciting enough the scientists collaborating on the project were even able to narrow down the date still further and suggest what time of year it had been as well.

The team of scientists was led by Alex Bayliss, of Sheffield University, acting as the 'Scientific Dating Co-ordinator' for English Heritage. However, aiming to get as accurate a date as possible, Bayliss worked in close conjunction with a team from Queen's University, Belfast, and timber experts from the Flag Fen Archaeological site in Cambridgeshire. The work took almost six months in total and resulted in the most accurate dating of prehistoric timbers ever to have taken place in the country.

The two main methods of dating, dendrochronology and radiocarbon dating, were used in association with each other, rather than separately, and the resulting figures were then subjected to a statistical technique first invented by an obscure clergyman, Thomas Bayes, in the first half of the eighteenth century. The first method, dendrochronology, was first developed at the beginning of the twentieth century by American astronomer Andrew Douglas. While researching the effects of sunspot activity on the earth's climate he discovered that the world's past weather patterns were recorded in the trees. He realised that the width of each tree ring corresponded to the level of rainfall the previous winter; wide rings in wet years and thin rings in years of less rainfall. By looking at the tree ring data stretching back over a number of decades a 'finger print' of the localised weather conditions was gradually built up. Within a short space of time the world's archaeologists realised the potential dating evidence offered by Andrew Douglas's methods and

the science of dendrochronology was born.

The system of tree ring dating is based on extracting data from the actual tree rings present in the timber. A sample of the timber is removed, at right angles to the tree rings, and the varying widths of the seasonal growth rings (the 'fingerprint') are then compared with a master record that has been compiled from known and dateable timber records. This technique can be highly accurate but it can only be used on certain species of tree and, due to the growth variants caused by climate, in specific regional areas. Luckily the available records for oak trees grown in northern Europe are extensive and a correct match seemed likely. However, tree ring dating relies upon a large number of tree rings actually being available: the larger the number of rings the more accurate it is likely to be. At the time the central stump was felled

Seahenge timbers partially submerged in the preservation tanks at Flag Fen. The bark, which aided the final dating process, can still be clearly seen. copyright - Barnwell's Timescape.

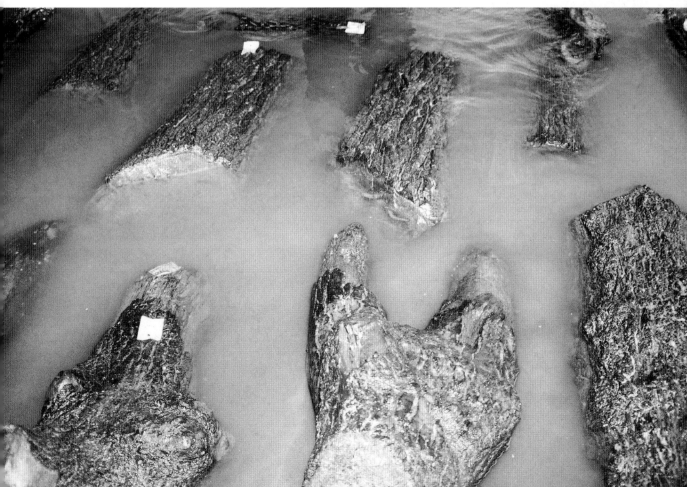

the tree was already nearly 150 years old but, unfortunately, due to the age and preservation of the timber, and the limited nature of the data for such an ancient period in history, a perfect match was not possible from the single sample. The oak's tree ring pattern loosely fitted several different areas of the available record. The best possible matches that could be suggested were 2050 BC, 2454 BC and 2019 BC.

The preservation tanks at Flag Fen have to be constantly cleaned to avoid the build up of harmful algae. copyright - Barnwell's Timescape.

Once these dates had been established the timbers then underwent radiocarbon dating. This method, also known as carbon 14 dating, is a scientific method that can be applied to all living things. While they are alive all living matter, be it a tree or a person, absorbs a radioactive isotope called carbon 14. When the object dies the carbon 14 level begins to decline, or decay. By comparing the amount of decay in the carbon 14 levels against modern control samples it is possible to establish when the subject died. However, even this highly scientific method is not perfect and it is only accurate to within plus or minus forty years.

As scientific techniques have advanced it has been able to improve upon this system to some extent.

Today there is available a technique known as 'High Precision Carbon Dating'. Although basically the same system as the original radiocarbon dating this improved method can date objects to within plus or minus twenty years. However, this method is not only difficult and expensive to carry out but also requires a much larger sample to be taken from the item to be dated. As techniques, and scientific ability, improve in the future it is hoped that this technique will become even more precise.

The timbers from Holme were subjected to just such radiocarbon dating techniques. Samples were taken from the tree rings approximately twenty years apart and analysed individually. The results suggested that the tree had died somewhere between 2200 BC and 2000 BC However, the team already knew that the samples differed in age by twenty years and they were able to eliminate the dendrochronological dates that fell outside the date range put forward by the carbon dating. It was at this point, when combining the data, that they applied the technique which has become known as 'Bayes Theorem'.

Bayes Theorem was the brainchild of one Thomas Bayes, the son of a nonconformist clergyman who was born in 1702. After an initial private education Thomas followed his father into the church and became a minister. However, Thomas' true interest lay in the world of mathematics and, although publishinglittle in his own life time, he did gain a solid reputation as a mathematician, being elected a member of the Royal Society in 1742. Thomas died in 1761, at the age of 59, while carrying out his duties as minister at the Presbyterian Chapel in Tunbridge Wells, Kent. While going through his papers a friend of Bayes, one Richard Price, discovered an unpublished paper entitled 'Essay towards solving a problem in the doctrine of chances'. Having read the paper, and finding its contents to be most intriguing, Richard Price submitted it to the Royal Society who published it in 1763.

The published paper outlined a new technique in the manipulation of statistics, known today as 'Bayes Theorem' or 'Bayesian Estimation', that enabled mathematicians to calculate exactly how true a proportion is likely to be. This theorem, unlike traditional techniques, allowed for the prior judgement and experience of the mathematician to be taken account of and added into the equation. The theorem proved popular with mathematicians and statisticians alike and was in common usage until early in the twentieth century. Unfortunately, in the light of perceived mathematical advances Bayes theorem began to be regarded with disdain by academics due to its inclusion in the calculation of experience based estimation; or guesswork as they would have it.

Today Bayes, ideas concerning the manipulation and calculation of statistics are once more beginning to be looked at with interest. The theorem, as well as being used in the Seahenge case, has been applied to improving customer services, court cases and even analysing the results of drug trials. It looks likely, taking into account past experience, that Bayes Theorem will be proving popular in the coming years.

The Bayesian mathematical model was applied to the data produced from both the tree ring dating and the radiocarbon dating of the Seahenge timbers. By recombining the probabilities contained in the two sets of data it was possible to produce a exceptionally narrow date range that corresponded with all the available information. In fact, the data strongly suggested that the main tree trunk from Holme had been felled in the year 2050 BC The finger posts were seen to have an extra growth ring that the main stump did not possess and it was therefore deduced that they had been felled the following year; 2049 BC The timber experts were able to go even further than this. By closely studying the partial growth ring on the outside of the main stump, and cross referencing thisto known growth patterns, they were able to state, with confidence, that the tree had been felled between April and June in the year 2050 BC; the finger posts had been felled the following spring.

Never before had archaeological science been able to correctly date such ancient timbers. All the scientists involved in the project were extremely pleased that it had been such a success.

Alex Bayliss, the projects *de facto* leader, was reported as saying that 'it is lovely to be able to get such an exact date for something built more than 4,000 years ago. This is the really important thing about this research: by using Bayesian mathematics we are bringing down prehistoric time-scales, ranges that cover decades or hundreds of years, to within that of human experience – a lifetime'.

Picture Overleaf - A replica of the type of bronze axe-head used to cut the timbers of Seahenge. copyright - Eastern Counties Newspapers Ltd.

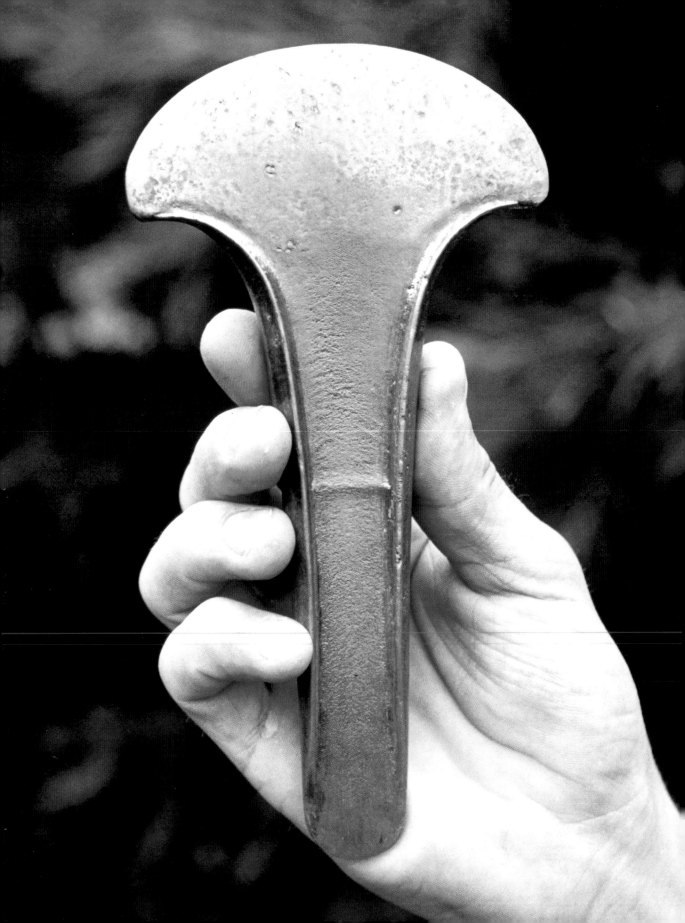

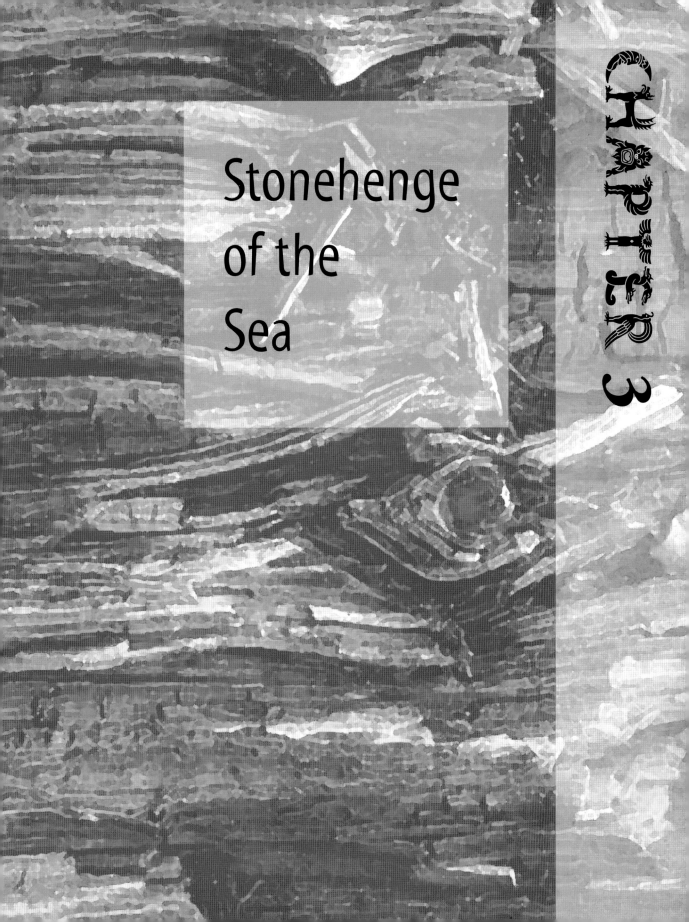

Stonehenge
of the
Sea

CHAPTER 3

Stonehenge of the Sea

The initial trial excavation and mapping of the site had revealed much additional information to the archaeologists and had shown that the site was of enormous importance. However, the expense involved with a full scale excavation, the inaccessible position of the circle and the fragile environmental nature of the land that it actually sat upon made any further work unlikely. It was decided that, in the best interests of all concerned, the Norfolk Wildlife Trust, English Heritage and the archaeologists, the monument should be left to the sea.

However, not everyone who had heard about the circle's emergence from the peat and the subsequent findings of the trial excavations agreed with this proposal. Certain sections of the archaeological community believed that the discovery was too important to be overlooked and that the site should be excavated, and if possible preserved, whatever the financial cost. They believed that the site was a fantastic opportunity to discover vast amounts about the early Bronze Age, their belief systems and their construction techniques. Other timber circles had been discovered in the past but none of them had ever been even partially as well preserved as the site at Holme Dunes. To let such a monument, with all its opportunities for the advancement of knowledge, simply disappear into the sea would be a criminal waste.

One of the leading critics of the decision by English Heritage to leave the circle in place was Dr Francis Pryor, a Director of Archaeology at Flag Fen in Cambridgeshire. Flag Fen is one of the foremost prehistoric sites in Britain and was established after the discovery, back in 1982, of a complete late Bronze Age village built on a huge platform of timbers that had been preserved in the fenland peat. The village, which once stood in the middle of a fenland mere, is also associated with a religious site and a huge palisade type structure built using over 60,000 individual timbers. Since its discovery, and on going excavation, Flag Fen has become one of the only centres in Britain that specialises in the preservation of ancient timbers. Dr Pryor has been involved with the Flag Fen site since its original discovery and is considered to be one of the country's leading experts in the field of ancient timbers. Further than this Dr Pryor is also the President for the Council for British Archaeology; an organisation that was soon mobilised to support his views concerning the circle at Holme.

Conveniently for Dr Pryor, and all those other people who supported the circles excavation, it was at this time that the media first got wind of the story and made it known to a wider audience. Although it has since been suggested that this was actually something more than a simple coincidence, the facts do not bear out such an interpretation. The story was already in the public domain and for those who knew where to look, which the journalists most certainly did, the information was readily available. Dr Pryor and his supporters simply made use of the opportunities presented to them and, in retrospect, used them more effectively than their opponents. However, when the story first broke it was hardly noticed. Instead of creating a great wave of public opinion it created barely a ripple.

The story was first made available to the public by Cath Saunt, acting in her role as District Producer For Local Radio, BBC Radio Norfolk, back in early December of 1998. At the time the monument was known simply as the 'Holme Timber Circle' and, although the trial excavation had just ended, little information was actually available on the discovery. 'I wrote a report', writes Cath, 'based on agency copy that was available on our computer wires. Not that many of us were particularly interested when the first report was written. . . it ran at the bottom of the bulletins and largely passed unnoticed'. Having run the story, and with no extra information available to them, Cath let the story go; but not before sending out a reporter to do a follow-up story.

The Storm Breaks

After the reports put out by Cath Saunt on BBC Radio Norfolk, the story of the circle went quiet for a while. Then, a little over a month later, the story broke for a second time. This time, however, it was under the banner headline 'Shifting sands yield Stonehenge of the Sea' and it was not in the local media but rather splashed across the front page of 'The Independent'. The journalist, Michael McCarthy, was environment correspondent for the paper and rather than just reporting the discovery he had also picked up on the fledgling debate that was beginning to rage over whether the site should be lifted. Describing the circle as 'one of the eeriest and most mysterious ancient monuments discovered in Britain' he focussed on the fact that unless action was taken the circle would be lost to the waves 'within two years'. McCarthy had also been in contact with Dr Pryor at Flag Fen and reported him as saying that the site 'is the most extraordinary archaeological discovery he has ever seen and it must be preserved'. McCarthy went on to quote Dr Pryor directly – 'I was staggered when I first saw it, I had goosepimples. It really was like stepping back 4,000 years. It's unique. It is of enormous international importance'.

It was this article, on the front page of a national newspaper, that first carried the picture of the timbers emerging from the water at Holme. This was the photograph, taken by Mark Brennand of the Norfolk Archaeological Unit, that was soon to be published in newspapers and magazines throughout the country. It had a profound effect on the public. The very fact that it lacked any sort of scale, showing as it did nothing but the circle, the beach and the water, left people feeling that this really was 'one of the eeriest and most mysterious ancient monuments discovered in Britain'. Coupled with the articles title reference to Stonehenge it was hardly surprising that the public quickly picked up on the story. A few days later Martin McCarthy wrote a follow up story entitled 'Stonehenge of sea will be left to ravages of tide' and the debate really began to heat up.

This follow up story dealt with the subject in a lot more depth than the original and had the advantage of involving both sides of the argument; those for and against preservation. Geoffrey Wainwright, the then chief archaeologist at English Heritage, was reported as saying that the circle could not be preserved in situ and that English Heritage had no plans at that time to lift and conserve the structure. Furthermore, Mr Wainwright went on to say that the project was 'a recording exercise, not a preservation exercise'. An English Heritage spokeswoman went further, stating that 'We feel it is sufficient to record what's there before it is eroded'.

However, despite beginning the article in such a manner Michael McCarthy went on to outline the opposition view in some depth. Senior archaeologists, he reported, were strongly opposed to the idea of leaving the site to the ravages of the sea and many believed that the monument was 'the most important ancient discovery made in Britain for many years'. Dr Francis Pryor, in his role as president of the Council for British Archaeology (rather than as an archaeological director of Flag Fen) was put in the position of figurehead for the protesters. 'I have to say', he is reported as saying, 'with a site of such importance, it is not enough just to record it. I think they ought to have another look at what their attitude to it is. If English Heritage', he concluded, 'say they've no plans to preserve it, then the question must be asked, who is responsible for preserving a site of such international importance?'.

This second article by Michael McCarthy was the first to highlight, and perhaps even add fuel to, the debate that was beginning to rage in archaeological circles. The circle was important, of that there was no doubt, but by describing it as 'the most important ancient discovery. . . for many years the archaeologists in favour of its excavation were ensuring that it received the maximum amount of media coverage. Furthermore, by acting under the guise of the Council for British Archaeology the protesters had automatically added a great deal of 'authority' to their argument. Had Dr Pryor simply presented his case as an interested archaeologist, with a specialist knowledge and fascination with the Bronze Age, one wonders whether his case would have been less well reported.

Nevertheless, the reports in *The Independent* had begun the debate; a debate that was to last, in one form or another, until the present time. The public suddenly found themselves intrigued by this piece of history reappearing on the Norfolk coast and the press were quick to follow up *the independent's* story. Cath Saunt, reporting for BBC Local Radio, World Service and News 24, hunted out her original story; the story that had passed almost unnoticed, and began to cover

the discovery from an in depth local angle. Cath was quick to visit the site, in co-operation with the archaeologists and site wardens, and her first reaction on seeing the circle is perhaps typical of many who ventured to the chill Norfolk coast in January of 1999. 'I remember', writes Cath, 'that while thinking it was small how intriguing it was to see such an old wooden structure so well preserved. When I was younger I did a spot of digging as a volunteer on archaeological sites in Buckinghamshire, therefore I was realistic yet astounded by the condition of the monument. The setting', continues Cath, 'rising as it did out of the sea was also impressive'.

Cath Saunt was not the only journalist to visit the site and reports of the circle's discovery soon began to fill column inches in both local and national newspapers. The monument caught the public's imagination and theories as to its original use soon began to find their way to the newspaper editors offices. In turn the newspapers gave the site more coverage and visitors to the site increased dramatically.

This increase in the number of visitors to the site was of concern to both the archaeologists and Norfolk Wildlife Trust wardens who cared for the Holme Dunes reserve. The winter bird populations at the reserve are of national importance and rely upon the winter solitude of the dunes and peat scarps for their food source. An increase in the number of visitors meant increased disturbance for the colonies and the chance that they would not be able to build up sufficient fat reserves to survive the bitter winter nights. The archaeologists too were worried about the visitors. The public numbers now present at the site far exceeded the normal average for the time of year and, set amid the delicate peat scarps, the monument was particularly susceptible to damage. Furthermore, reports began to emerge that some members of the public, not being satisfied with just viewing the circle, were actually removing stray pieces of timber as souvenirs.

In a letter to John Lorimer, dated the 12th of January, Brian Ayers, the Principal Field Archaeologist for the Norfolk Archaeological Unit, expressed his concern at 'the problems which have been caused by the publicity of the last few days'. Mr Ayers went on state that the archaeological unit 'did not issue a press release concerning the site. The story had already been covered in the archaeological press some six weeks ago and at least three times on local radio.

We are not anxious', continued Brian Ayers, 'for further coverage. We have issued a statement which we hope will be effective. We are emphasising the fragility of the local environment when fielding enquiries and are extremely anxious to work closely with Gary Hibberd (the site warden) on all future contact with the media'.

It is interesting to note that the Norfolk Archaeological Unit state that they did not issue a statement to the press concerning the circle. The find

since the raising of the Mary Rose, the excavation of the Rose theatre and the discovery of the Roman Sarcophagus in London had an archaeological story received such treatment.

Despite the Archaeological Unit's wish to limit the publicity attracted by the circle, and the subsequent unseasonal number of visitors to the Holme Dunes Nature Reserve, their troubles were only just beginning. Two days after the letter to John Lorimer the Eastern Daily Press, one of England's leading regional daily

had already been reported on in the academic archaeological press; which led to it being available to Cath Saunt on a news wire service, and had been reported on Local Radio (Cath's reports) but had not been promoted by the archaeologists. However, when approached by 'The Independent' the Norfolk Archaeological unit had, without a second thought, released to them the photograph taken by Mark Brennand. It has since been suggested that the unit administration felt that there was no harm in such a move; after all they expected it to be used in conjunction with a minor story hidden deep in the paper's inner pages. The fact that it appeared splashed over the front page of a national daily newspaper came as a great surprise to all those involved; not

newspapers, issued a four page 'souvenir pullout' that covered the story of the circle. Headlining a 'special report' by Norfolk journalist David Barrett the souvenir pullout emphasised the debate about the circle's future that was already raging. Although running a small boxed report, at the bottom of page two, that asked the public to stay away from the site the souvenir pullout ensured that the circle, or 'Seahenge' as it had now been christened, would remain at the forefront of public debate. If anyone in East Anglia had been previously unaware of the circle they could not remain in ignorance for long.

In fact the souvenir pullout probably achieved exactly the opposite effect of the one the journalist proposed to advocate. Instead of keeping the public away from the site the following weekend saw a marked increase in visitor numbers at Holme Dunes.

However, the souvenir pullout did have a marked effect upon the debate as to whether the monument should be left to the sea or excavated and saved for science and posterity. Running the story of the debate on page four, under the banner headline 'The big question is: should it be saved?', the journalist outlined the main points that had to be considered. He also interviewed Dr Brian Ayers, from the Norfolk Archaeological Unit, and attempted to gauge his opinion. 'You can always pull timbers out of the ground', Dr Ayers is reported as saying, 'and fire chemicals at them for 25 years to preserve them. But what meaning will the monument have if it is divorced from the landscape? It would just be a pile of old wood in a museum. That is the debate we must have'.

Despite Bryan Ayers reluctance to commit himself one way or the other the newspaper article really gave a boost to the debate at the local level. Letters both for and against excavation began to appear in the Eastern Daily Press and pressure began to mount upon the authorities to save the circle. How could they possibly leave what had been described as an 'extraordinary discovery' to the mercy of the waves? Was it not their job to preserve just such sites for the nation?

A Change Of Heart

Two days later Philip Carr-Gomm, an individual with an interest in the future of the circle, e-mailed Sir Jocelyn Stevens, the chairman of English Heritage. The reply to Mr Carr-Gomm's enquiry was posted on the internet for all to see. In reply to Mr Carr-Gomm's question concerning English Heritage's proposed policy concerning the circle Sir Jocelyn Stevens wrote:-

'We are considering the possibility of preserving the circle but that option presents a number of difficulties not least because the timbers are submerged by the sea for up to 23 hours each day. The likelihood of being able to preserve the circle where it stands is remote and we can see little point in doing so. The second option is to lift the timbers, conserve them and re-erect the monument on terra firma at a suitable location. This would be a major operation which preliminary estimates of cost put at 500K'.

Sir Jocelyn then continues 'For these reasons we currently think that a full recording exercise, before the timbers are left to the mercy of the waves, is the realistic option. Nevertheless, we are exploring the preservation options whilst we await the dating of the timbers'. Sir Jocelyn, in a final note concerning the environmental impact of the discovery, once again re-emphasises that the release of information to the media was not the doing of the archaeologists involved. 'The premature publicity', he writes, 'given to the discovery – which was not of our doing – has resulted in numbers of visitors attempting to wade out to the site and English Nature has expressed their deep concern to the Norfolk Archaeological Unit on account of disturbance caused to the birds. This', he concluded, 'will need to be taken into account in any future plans'.

In fact, the representative of English Nature and the Norfolk Wildlife Trust actually working at Holme Dunes, Gary Hibbert, had gone even further. Having seen the disturbance and disruption to his beloved bird species caused by the discovery he is reported in the Eastern Daily Press as saying "I hope they are going to preserve this monument. I hope they are going to take it away".

It was beginning to look likely that Gary Hibbert would soon have his wish granted. In a matter of weeks English Heritage had gone from stating that the project would definitely be 'a recording exercise, not a preservation exercise' to 'exploring the preservation options'. However, before any real decisions could be taken funding would have to be made available. Norfolk County could not afford it, being unwilling to fund even the trial excavation in late 1998, and neither could the Museums service (in itself funded by the County Council). If the monument was to be saved then the money would have to be made available by the government, through the government funded quango English Heritage.

However, under pressure from the media, the public, archaeologists such as Dr Francis Pryor, English Nature and the Norfolk Wildlife trust the powers that be at English Heritage began to realise that by ignoring the plight of the circle they were courting a publicity disaster. If they refused to make funds available then they would be attacked as uncaring and short sighted. Their job was to protect our heritage; why were they not doing it? Finally, at the beginning of May

1999 it was made known to the media and the public that a decision had been made; English Heritage would pay to excavate and lift the monument. Work was scheduled to begin on Wednesday the 26th of May 1999 and last about one month.

The reaction to the decision to lift the site was greeted with mixed feelings by many of those closely connected with the site. Gary Hibbert, the Trust warden, believed the decision was a wise one. After more than 500 people visited the site over the Spring Bank Holiday weekend alone Gary was reported as saying 'Moving the circle will take a lot of pressure off the site'. Gary's opinion was soon backed by Dr Brian Ayers from the Norfolk Archaeological Unit. Although originally unwilling to commit himself to supporting any one course of action Dr Ayers was quickly reported as saying "I think this was the right decision and we should act to move it as soon as possible. We have an immediate problem because of the threat from the elements – the last thing anyone wants is to wake up one morning to discover it has been washed away".

At this point it appeared that the media, backed by public opinion, had actually changed English Heritage's policy concerning the circle and won a victory over the authorities. Supporting the views of archaeologists like Dr Pryor they had pushed forward a common sense decision and overthrown the stuffy indifference of the bureaucrats. However, as one dose of media 'spin' began to fade, and with the public interest in the monument beginning to wane, there seemed no reason for the story to keep filling column inches each week. Then, just as the decision to excavate was made public, the media discovered a new spin; not everybody wanted the monument to be lifted.

Suddenly, instead of arguing the case to lift the circle, and reporting on the protesters who wanted it excavated, the journalists could follow the story of the fight to halt that process. With feelings running high a good story was almost inevitable and the involvement of the Druids and spiritualists only gave the fleet street reporters even more to savour. The tabloid hacks, laptops in the one hand, mobile phones in the other, decamped and headed for the Norfolk coast. It was going to be an interesting summer.

Without the intervention of the numerous newspaper, radio and television reports, and the subsequent public outcry, it is unlikely that the debate would have reached far beyond the halls of academia. In fact, without the public's involvement it is probable that the circle would have remained untouched. However, the public awareness of the monument did not simply mean that public opinion lent weight to Dr Pryor's argument. Far from it; the public's involvement in the growing debate was seen as unwelcome by many of those involved with the site and, with growing pressure from increased visitor numbers at the nature reserve itself, it appeared likely that the authorities would have to act. With the threat of damage to both the nature reserve and the monument growing daily, and the media questioning the decisions of English Heritage at the most senior level, the debate swung in Dr Pryor's favour. Funds were made available, a team assembled and the date for excavation set. Seahenge was going to be removed.

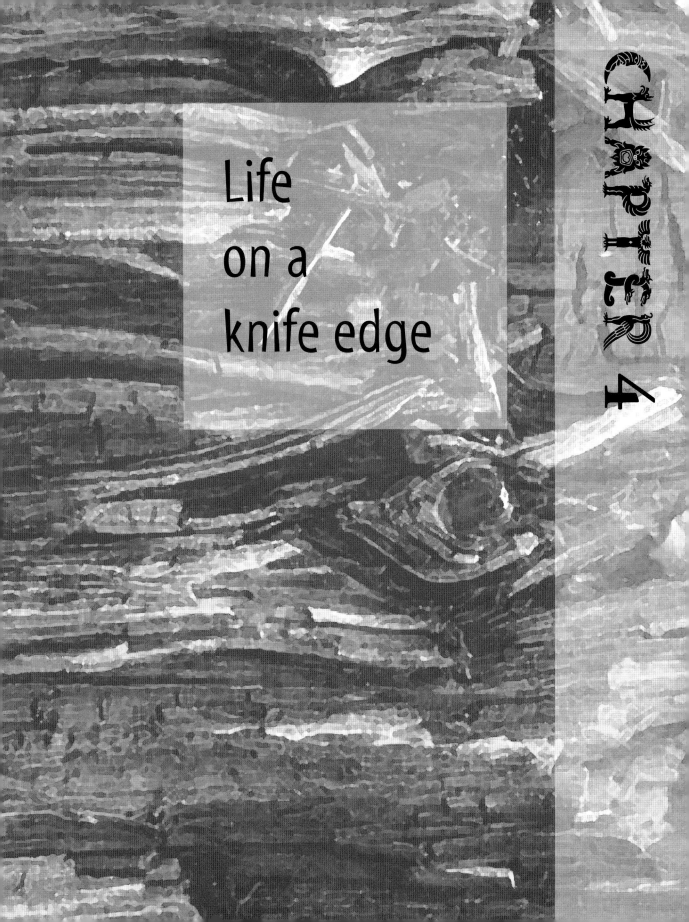

Life on a knife edge

The original location of Seahenge was one of the many factors that made the discovery and excavation of the monument such a fraught affair. The circle itself was situated between the high and low water marks on the beach at the Holme Dunes Nature Reserve. The site at Holme is managed by the Norfolk Wildlife Trust and is a site of great importance for wildlife and, most especially, birdlife.

The site is of such importance, and of such a sensitive nature that it has been designated a National Nature Reserve, a Site of Special Scientific Interest (SSSI) and a Wetland of International Importance under the Ramsar convention. These designations do provide certain legal protections to the nature reserve, though of limited actual usage, and in addition certain species found at the site, such as the Natterjack toad, receive additional legal protection from both British and European law. In effect, the site is of national and international importance and one of the most sensitive environmental areas on the whole North Norfolk coast. However, just to complicate the matter the Norfolk Wildlife Trust does not actually own the land that the circle was discovered on.

In normal circumstances the land between the high water mark and the low water mark, or 'foreshore' as it is commonly known, is the property of the Crown. However, in the case of Holme this ownership had been granted by the Crown to the local Le Strange family. The actual grant had taken place in the thirteenth century and, in exchange for services to the monarch the family had also been granted the title of Lord High Admiral of the Wash in perpetuity. The story is that as far as the gentleman could ride on a white charger and throw a spear, where it landed was the extent of his boundary. The dunes and beach at Holme fell well within this boundary and had been leased out to the Norfolk Wildlife Trust on a long term basis. In effect, at least technically, anything discovered on the beach, the monument included, belonged to the Le Strange family.

Although the site is owned by the Le Strange family it is the Norfolk Wildlife Trust who actually manage and control the physical area around the monument and the circle's emergence added a new and unexpected threat to the site's wildlife. The reserve is home to many species that depend on the beach habitat for the means to survive and any additional disturbances in the area can easily prove devastating. With the reserve already under pressure and threatened by both the sea itself and the rising problems of increased visitor numbers the circle's emergence, and subsequent national publicity, was less than welcome.

One of the many rare and endangered species that rely upon the habitat provided by Holme Dunes copyright - A.D. Images.

The threat to the nature reserve from the sea is very real, and one than can be appreciated by anyone who has spent any length of time on the East Anglian coast. Sand bars and dunes that are there one year can be entirely gone twelve months later and new ones can have appeared several miles down the coast. Entire sections of cliff disappear each winter and whole villages and towns have, in the past, fallen prey to the sea. Further to the south, on the Suffolk coast, the town of Dunwich, formerly one of the Anglo

Saxon capitals of the region and a major mediaeval seaport, has been entirely consumed by the waves, while to the south of this, at Orford, the Ness continues to grow in length each year. The sands are eternally shifting and by the time a map is published it is usually already out of date.

The threat from the sea at the Holme Dunes Reserve is best described by Bill Boyd, an official of the Norfolk Wildlife Trust, in a statement issued in June 1999:-

'Sand, shingle and mud have been transported by sea and wind action to form the substrates of the site and dune and saltmarsh vegetation have developed on these over many years. Now the same processes that built up these deposits are working to remove them. Beach levels have dropped by 1-2 metres in the past ten years allowing larger waves to impact higher up the beach and directly on the dunes during storm tides.

One theory explaining this is rather complex, but points to the construction of a mile long sea wall in the 1860s. This shut the sea out of the vast saltmarsh behind the dunes and allowed it to be 'reclaimed' for grazing and, later, agriculture. Water flowed out of this saltmarsh into the open sea and interrupted the drift of sediments along the coast to create a large area of deposits as a delta bulging out from the shore. The water was shallower over this delta which protected the coast on either side from the damaging attacks of storm tides. . . Shutting the sea out of the saltmarsh by construction of the seawall meant that this delta was no longer so well fed by sediments and it reduced in size. As it has reduced so has the protection it offered to the coastline. . . This lack of sediment input and impact of storm tides has caused the beach levels to drop so exposing the dunes to direct attack by the sea. Even if the man made seawall were to be removed and natural processes allowed to build up the delta again, it could be very many years before the system started to go into reverse'.

Unfortunately, this lowering in the level of the beach has exposed a material that is, if anything, even more fragile than the sand dunes. The timber circle itself is not buried in sand but rather in a thick layer of peat. This peat, which overlays a clay base, was laid down when the area was a waterlogged marshland. Its permanently semi-wet state means that peat contains very little oxygen and, as a consequence, the micro-organisms that cause vegetable matter to decay find it a difficult environment to inhabit. This means that almost any organic material that is sealed in by the peat will survive for long periods of time in a spectacular state of preservation.

In the past, most especially in Denmark, many peat bogs have been found to contain sacrificed human remains. The bodies normally surface when the peat is being harvested and before the introduction of modern dating techniques their remarkable condition led many to believe that they were the victims of murders or accidents in relatively modern times. However, modern analysis has shown that the bodies are much more ancient than at first believed and that the chemicals present in the peat bogs themselves, combined with an almost sealed environment, helped in their natural mummification. These bodies, often over a thousand years old, have been so well preserved by the peat that it is sometimes even possible to identify what their last meal consisted of. Although such finds in this country are rare they have occurred and it is likely that others still remain to be discovered. If the peat can preserve something as organically complex as the human body then the oak timbers that made up Seahenge would not present it with any problems.

However, peat is a delicate material and the lowering in the level of the beach now means that it is further exposed to the effects of the sea. Combined with the scouring effects of the sand being washed backwards and forwards over its surface the peat is being rapidly worn away. It was this process that brought the timber circle to light and the self same process that would have eventually destroyed it. It is also the process that will change the nature reserve forever.

It must be understood that Holme Dunes is not simply just another nature reserve; it is a unique habitat that is one of the few remaining havens forseveral rare species of bird life. The actual area around the circle is home to such wading birds as Sanderling, Knot, Grey Plover and Bar Tailed Godwit and these are regularly present on the beach in internationally important numbers. Many of the species actually breed in the Arctic, returning to Holme to over winter in late summer, however, these are not the only birds for whom the reserve is of vital importance. Between spring and early summer the reserve becomes home to many other breeding colonies of birds, such as the Oystercatcher, Little Tern and Ringed Plover, and these species often make their nests in the dunes immediately surrounding the circle.

Such breeding colonies are very easily disturbed by man and although the Trust wardens attempt to cordon off the most densely populated breeding grounds it is inevitable that many breeding pairs are disturbed by visitors to the site. In a normal year the early summer is usually a fairly quiet time for visitors and breeding colonies tend to go largely undisturbed. Unfortunately, the early summer of 1999 was not going to be a quiet time for the reserve.

The many hundreds of extra visitors who were attracted to the site by the discovery of the circle caused immense disturbance to the breeding colonies and, albeit unwittingly, damaged the actual physical environment. The peat beds which surrounded the circle are extremely fragile and even the footfalls of an extra hundred visitors caused them to be damaged. Although liable to be eventually destroyed by the sea their destruction was hastened, with untold long term effects, by the visitors to the circle. In the summer the breeding colonies were disturbed, reducing their chances of successfully reproducing, and in winter the waders were constantly unsettled while feeding; threatening their ability to lay down the layers of fat needed to survive the freezing nights. Whether the visitors liked it or not they were destroying the environment that many of them believed they were helping to protect.

The Norfolk Wildlife Trust were immediately aware that the situation could, very easily, become an environmental disaster. Gary Hibbert, the Norfolk Wildlife Trust site warden, was passionate about protecting the site from the additional attention caused by the circle's emergence and was reported as saying that he 'hoped that they (the archaeologists) would take it away'. The national media coverage that the circle was receiving was encouraging many hundreds of extra visitors to the site. These visitors were also there for only one purpose; to see the much talked about timber circle. Unlike the vast majority of the reserve's normal visitors these additional sightseers had little interest in the wildlife that surrounded them and perhaps did not realise that they were helping to destroy something just as precious, and as ancient, as the circle itself; the ecosystem. In an attempt to stem the flow of visitors and limit the damage the Trust asked the press to 'respect the sensitivity of the site and its significance for internationally important species'.

This plea for press moderation from the site's managers fell, unfortunately, on deaf ears. The popular press continued to hype the story and only the local papers, including the Eastern Daily Press in its souvenir pullout, ran any stories

asking the public to stay away. The pleas for sightseers to steer clear of the area made by the Wildlife Trust were soon supported by pleas from the archaeologists working on the site. Brian Ayers from the Norfolk Archaeological unit was quick to point out that 'if people visit the monument in any numbers it will destroy the peat and that will destroy the monument'. 'if they go there', he continued, 'it is unlikely they will see it because it's under water most of the time. They will damage the site and the natural environment, so I would ask them to please stay away'.

Whether the combined pleas of the reserve's wardens and the archaeologists actually had any effect is unknown. Visitor numbers to the site did dramatically increase, over 500 arriving over a single weekend, but whether they would have increased still further had the appeals not been made is a question open to debate. As it was the site did suffer additional damage by the increase in visitor numbers and the breeding colonies were disturbed. However, the extent of this damage, the real long term effects of the discovery, have yet to be fully assessed.

The final word on the environmental impact of the circle's discovery must be given to Bill Boyd of the Norfolk Wildlife Trust. In a statement issued in June 1999, at the height of the excavation controversy, Bill Boyd states that

'On a coastline that is busy with human leisure activity, wildlife is under great pressure even on nature reserves. The primary purpose of the Norfolk Wildlife Trust Holme Dunes National Nature Reserve is to maintain populations of the key plants and animals and to maintain the habitats in good conditions. Norfolk Wildlife Trust knows that people and groups have different views on the future of the timber circle, but needs to point out that there is something else extremely valuable at stake here, in particular the waders which have been visiting this shore to breed, rest or feed for centuries, and which may be damaged by even well intentioned visitors, whether they are for or against the excavation or merely curious.

To those people who respect nature – the Earth and its ecological systems – there is much to be concerned about in the current disagreements over the circle's timbers. These must be quickly resolved if the natural human interest in the ancient circle is not to interfere with the continued operation of these wader's strategies for migration and survival – which are also fascinating and mysterious. Knot and other waders spend their lives on an energetic knife edge – a balance between the availability of quality undisturbed feeding areas and the need for energy to undertake great migration flights and to survive freezing weather; the beach at Holme is part of the chain of sites that maintain them'.

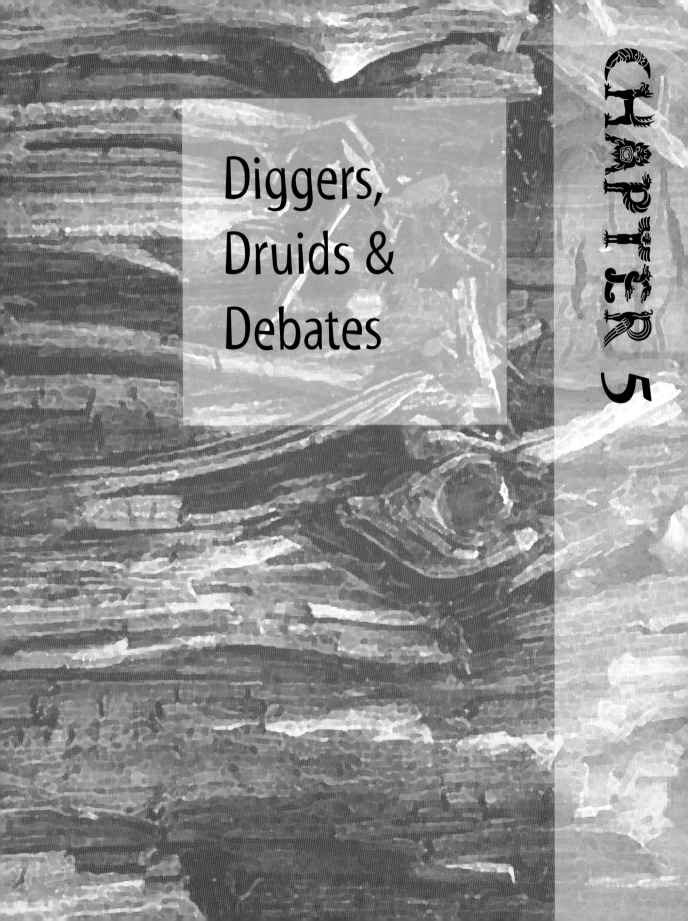

Diggers, Druids & Debates

CHAPTER 5

Almost as soon as English Heritage had made public the decision to excavate the circle at Holme Dunes, at the beginning of May 1999, they began to realise that it was not as popular as they had at first hoped. Admittedly they had the wholehearted support of people such as Dr Francis Pryor, John Lorimer and Gary Hibbert, but they soon discovered that the opposition to the circle's excavation was as strong, if not stronger, than the opposition to it being left to the sea. As far back as the Eastern Daily Press 'souvenir pullout', in January 1999, local people had begun to argue for the circle to be left in peace and in the weeks between making the decision public and the excavations beginning the strength of opposition began to grow. In many respects English Heritage had jumped from the frying pan into the fire.

Local opposition to the circle's removal had grown steadily since the debate began to rage back in January of 1999 and over the intervening months it had taken on a more organised form. The village of Holme was justly proud of its new found fame and wanted to preserve what it considered its own heritage. Although not everyone agreed on how this should best be achieved, many believing that excavation was the right answer, a growing body of local people felt that the circle should stay in place.

The circle had become something of a focal point for the villagers; a monument that they felt 'belonged' to the village; almost as much as the village church or village hall. Stephanie Middleton, bar manager in one of the local pubs and local resident with a strong interest in the village, speaks for many when she writes that the villagers felt 'that we had something special in the village, a feeling of a presence when you stood by the circle'. Geoff Needham, a long time visitor to the beach and Chairman of the Holme Parish Council, also felt a deep connection with the site. 'On first seeing the circle', writes Geoff, 'it was as if I should not have been looking at it, and that it was trying not to be seen, a bit weird really'.

Geoff Needham, as a prominent local resident, was one of those who soon began to spearhead the campaign to stop the lifting and removal of the circle and soon became something of a local figurehead for the campaign. 'I felt very strongly', he writes, 'about the historical significance, and importance the circle is to our heritage. We are but custodians', he continues, 'and have a duty to protect it for future generations'. Geoff Needham and many other local people felt as if their views had been overlooked by both English Heritage and the media. They had not been asked to give their opinions and no one seemed interested in what they believed should happen to the circle. News of the decision to excavate came again via the media and was, according to Stephanie Middleton, 'utterly devastating'. She firmly believes that those involved with the decision making process were simply 'power people, bulldozing ahead without real consideration for anything or anybody'. Unfortunately, for English Heritage, Stephanie was not alone in her view.

As the weeks passed the residents of Holme were joined in their opposition to the proposed excavation by many other people from throughout East Anglia and Britain as a whole. Amongst these was Sam Jones, a Norfolk woman who later led the 'Friends of Seahenge' campaign, and deeply felt that the removal of the timbers before they had been properly studied in situ would be a grave mistake. Sam was simply one of the first of many spiritualists attracted to this enigmatic site. The concept of the removal of such an ancient monument, believed by many to be of deep spiritual significance, touched many a raw nerve and in a short time it began to appear that the protesters, far from being in the minority as originally portrayed, were actually the majority. This was soon borne out by a local media phone-in debate which resulted in over 6000 calls; 5000 of which opposed the excavation. English Heritage began to realise that they could no longer simply overlook the views of the local people.

In what the local people believed was bowing to overwhelming public pressure English Heritage agreed to attend a public meeting, called by Geoff Needham and the parish council, in Holme Village Hall on the evening of the 25 May. In an attempt to relieve some of the growing local pressure that was building in the days leading up to the meeting English Heritage, on the 24 May, issued a statement to the press and public. Hoping to allay local fears English Heritage made it plain that the circle would go on display close to where it had been discovered; somewhere in western Norfolk. However, this would only happen after the timbers had been lifted and taken away for preservation at Flag Fen near Peterborough.

Unfortunately, the English Heritage statement, far from releasing the tension, appeared to have just the opposite effect. Local people had anticipated going along to the public meeting to discuss what was actually going to happen to the monument. Stephanie

Middleton, herself a concerned local resident who planned to attend the gathering, was 'under the impression that it was to discuss whether the circle should stay'. Now, however, it appeared that the authorities had already decided upon the fate of the circle and that the excavation would begin the following day (May 26) come what may.

This revelation came as a bitter blow to many of the local residents. Geoff Needham, speaking for many, was reported as saying that he now believed the meeting would be little more than paying 'lip service' to the local peoples' concerns. Mr Needham went on to say that 'we thought they had called the meeting finally to listen to what we have got to say. Now', he continued, 'it turns out that they have already made up their minds. There are a large number of local people who think that the circle should not be touched'. However, despite his concerns over the fate of the circle, and his disappointment at the attitude of the authorities, Geoff Needham decided, along with dozens of other interested parties, to carry on with the meeting and listen to what was said.

A Stormy Meeting

The meeting in Holme village hall that evening was a crowded affair. The hall was crammed with local residents, protesters and journalists who had all come along to hear what English Heritage and the Norfolk Archaeological Unit had to say. The meeting was headed by Philip Walker, the head of English Heritage Eastern Region, who outlined the reasoning behind the decision to excavate the circle. The basis of English Heritage's decision was founded upon the belief that if the circle was not excavated it would soon be lost to the sea. The site was of great importance, much could be learned from it, and its loss would be a major blow. Excavation would begin the following day.

This reiteration of the position of both the archaeologists and English Heritage was not well received by the majority of those present at the meeting. True, there were some who felt that this action would be for the best, but a far greater number of those present felt, in the words of Stephanie Middleton, that they were being 'bulldozed again'. The attitude of those people who spoke for English Heritage and the archaeologists was seen as

uncompromising. Geoff Needham felt that they were 'not there to listen to local concern, or to do any deals, but to tell us what was in the best interests of archaeology'. Geoff felt that 'the speakers on the platform came over as very arrogant, and that they knew best' and that this view was shared by many others who attended the meeting.

The rest of the meeting was, at times, a stormy affair. Person after person got up to express their concern at the circle's removal and the high handed attitude of the authorities. Many felt that not enough research had been done on the part of English Heritage concerning the local coastal erosion. The local people, those that had known the beach and foreshore for decades, were, they believed, in a better position to judge the true threat to the monument. Others felt that the removal of the circle from Holme would divorce it from its true context and lead to the loss of much valuable information concerning its positioning in the landscape. Far better, said some, to leave it in place so that further work could be carried out on the structure before any long term plans were made for its future.

Cath Saunt, reporting on the meeting for the BBC, was in a good position to judge the true feelings of both protesters and archaeologists. 'The first meeting', she writes, 'at Holme village hall was antagonistic and heated. (The) villagers said they were only consulted the day before excavation began – and even then it appeared to them cursory, the decision to dig a *fait accompli*. Many others were furious', she continues, 'that a chunk of the centre oak had been cut out with a chainsaw the year before for dating purposes'.

In the eyes of many it was this act, the use of a chainsaw on the timbers, that summed up the attitude of the authorities. In the words of Geoff Needham it was an 'act of vandalism' and one that did not inspire confidence in the future safety of the circle in their hands. 'I could see', writes Cath Saunt, 'both sides. The archaeologists saw excavation as a unique opportunity to find out more about that period of history. They thought the site was a missing link or possibly the earliest example of that kind of structure that have been built from pre-history to the present day. The locals felt', she continues, 'it had been there for thousands of years and was integral to the landscape. . .

The argument – excavate or it will be destroyed by the sea, they thought, was simplistic'.

The meeting at Holme village hall broke up after several hours and few of those who were present felt that anything useful had been achieved or any of the local concerns properly addressed. Many of the local residents came to the conclusion that the meeting had been a waste of time and that English Heritage, much as they expected in the days before the gathering, had no intention of taking their views into consideration. The excavation would go ahead, come what may, and any opposition would be,disregarded. Whatever English Heritage had hoped to achieve by calling the meeting all they had actually managed to do was harden the views of the opposition against them.

This view, that the meeting was little more than a sham, was, in the eyes of many of those involved, soon validated. The next morning, watched by interested locals, the archaeologists made their way down to the beach at Holme to begin their excavation and removal of the timber circle. Geoff Needham, in the interests of accuracy and posterity, took it upon himself to record much of what went on, both then and over the following weeks. Armed with a video camera he followed the actions of the archaeologists as they began to dig away the top layer of sand. This sand had accumulated around the timbers and the archaeologists used it to fill the sandbags that they would use to try and protect their operations from the sea; in all Geoff shot over nine hours of video footage.

However, if the Norfolk Archaeological Unit and English Heritage believed that they were going to be allowed to carry out what many of the protesters termed 'vandalism' without any opposition they were sadly mistaken. The leading protesters were already getting themselves organised, establishing their contacts and generally preparing to meet, and defeat, the archaeologists on their own ground. They were preparing themselves to carry out a prolonged campaign of peaceful protest; a campaign that would, at the very least, highlight what they perceived as the overbearing and inconsiderate attitude of the authorities and, at best, halt the excavation altogether.

One major part of this campaign was spearheaded by Sam Jones, a local youth worker, painter and spiritual healer, who felt strongly that none of the academics involved with the decision making process had taken any account of the spiritual and religious aspects of the monument. Having heard about the circle's existence from the local media Sam was devastated at the news that the circle was to be removed. She quickly made her way to Holme, being present at the meeting in the village hall, and had deep feelings about the special nature of the circle after her first visit out onto the dunes. 'Rather than seeing the site', she writes

45

'it was the feelings of a very calm feminine energy. It's a sign of natural harmony and thus only nature can decide its fate. I seek to honour nature and spirit above science", she continues, "and feel that science has led us astray and threatens our existence'.

Sam Jones was outraged at the way she felt the views of the local people, and those who felt a spiritual connection to the site, were treated by the authorities and determined that it would not end with the meeting in the village hall.

'I had never protested before', she writes, 'I hadn't got a clue what to do and how to do it but I felt I must do something'. Feeling that the national media had tended to ignore the story since the original debate concerning the excavation back in January Sam began by phoning around the various newspapers, radio stations and television companies in the hope of 'getting a wider audience' to appreciate the new situation. However, this was before any real active protest had taken place at Holme Dunes and the media, thinking the story already over and done with, took little notice of Sam's efforts. Frustrated at the media's disinterest, but still in need of support and advice, she decided to try a different approach.

As a healer and spiritualist Sam Jones had previously come into contact with several organisations that professed to represent many of the older pagan religions of Britain, in particular the Druids, and it was to these groups, and their associated organisations, that she now turned to for support. Her initial telephone calls met with a polite and interested response and, after explaining the situation in Norfolk and the actions of the authorities in connection with the circle, she was soon put in touch with veteran tree spokesperson, Buster Nolan.

Buster, a committed conservationist from Essex, has been leading an on-going campaign to draw public attention to the fact that most of our native British trees, in particular the English oak, are dying. In the process of his campaign Buster has been in close contact with several of the Druid churches who share his concerns for the environment. As a result, and in recognition of his work, the Council of British Druid Orders (COBDO), which represents seventeen independent Druid orders and claims membership of approximately twenty thousand people, invited Buster to Stonehenge to help them celebrate the traditional summer solstice oak ceremony. Although not a Druid himself Buster has retained contact with the organisation and has acted as an ex officio representative upon several occasions.

When Sam Jones contacted Buster about the fate of the circle at Holme she was immediately offered any help that she required and that was within Buster's power to give. He felt that the circle's emergence from the sea was of great importance and, as a builder of timber circles himself, including one that contained an inverted oak at its centre, he already felt a personal connection to the site. Furthermore, Buster resolved to take an active interest in the site's protection and called upon the COBDO to add their support.

Rollo Maughfling, Archdruid of Stonehenge and Glastonbury and representative of the Council of British Druid Orders, was soon made aware of the situation by Buster and pledged the support of the COBDO as and when it was needed. 'When the news of the discovery first broke in the press', writes Rollo Maughfling, 'it was adjudged by my colleagues that this was one such issue on which we could not remain silent'. Mr Maughfling well remembers his initial contacts with Buster Nolan and was impressed by his enthusiasm for the circle and his perception. 'From the beginning', writes Mr Maughfling, 'he (Buster) rightly foresaw that the authorities were going to intervene in the fate of Seahenge, and not in any manner that either local people or religious interests were going to find acceptable. I can well remember his enthusiastic descriptions of the site over the telephone'.

However, after Buster made his initial visits to the site he came away with a less than favourable opinion of many of the archaeologists involved; an opinion he was quick to relay to Rollo Maughfling. 'He said, over his initial conversations with the archaeologists', writes Mr Maughfling, 'that 'they don't seem interested in what its for or why it's where it is, they just want to rip it up and pack it off to some museum somewhere where no one can use it and all that will ever happen is that it gathers dust'.

Peaceful Protests

On the 21st of May the archaeologists began the excavation by removing the top layers of accumulated sand, filling sandbags and attempting to shore up the site against the tides that covered it for the majority of each day. Their aim was to remove the outer circle of posts, or at least a large number of them, so that they could get the heavy diggers in close enough to lift the central tree stump. Its large size, and the fact that it was embedded in the clay layer beneath the peat, meant that the area around it had to be fully excavated before any attempt could be made to lift it individually. However, from almost the moment the archaeologists set to work they found their task hampered by an increasing number of protesters.

To begin with the protesters were very few in number. Buster Nolan and Sam Jones, who both lived some distance away, were present as much as was possible and Geoff Needham, who lives in the village itself, was on hand to record the actions of the archaeologists whenever time allowed. As the days passed, and news of the proposed excavation spread, other protesters arrived to lend their support to the campaign to halt the excavation. Some stayed only a few hours, others for several days and a hardened few returned time and again. None of the protesters entered into the debate lightly; all had thought through the consequences of their actions.

Among the ranks of the more frequent visitors to the circle were Hazel and Des Crow. Hazel, a spiritualist and environmental campaigner from nearby Cambridgeshire, was well aware of the delicate nature of the nature reserve but felt, on balance, that the circle was of more immediate importance. 'I had a number of problems with this protest', she writes, 'Firstly as a wildlife campaigner and environmentalist, I did have initial concerns about the bird sanctuary. However, their arguments over peat beds etc. were not strong enough. If the circle was to be washed away, then so would the peat beds – and eventually the birds would leave'

Hazel's concerns about the site were shared by Des Crow (known simply as Crow to his friends) but he too felt that the circles fate was of overriding importance. At the time that the decision to excavate was made public Crow was actually spending some time at Lodge Farm in Surrey where a stone circle was being reconstructed. 'A message was passed onto me from Norfolk resident 'Sam' (Sam Jones)', writes Crow, 'she had attended a public meeting at Holme and was very concerned about the actions of English Heritage and their plans to start removing the oak circle. Local people were outraged and I shared their concern – I decided to make my way up to Norfolk'.

The first time each of the protesters saw the circle it was a deeply spiritual event for them; as it was for most people who ventured out to Holme Dunes. The published photographs had been misleading and everyone expected the monument to be much larger than it actually was. Hazel writes that 'My reaction upon first seeing the circle was surprise at how small it was, but then on entering, how vast it feels and how powerful'. This feeling, that the circle was physically small but, on another level, quite massive, was shared by both Crow and many of the local people. With the flat expanse of beach stretching away in either direction, under the wide North Norfolk sky, the circle itself could easily be lost in the windswept landscape, yet, once you were standing in it, it felt like the centre of the world.

On their first visits to the oak circle both Crow and Hazel found themselves sharing the monument with the archaeologists from the Norfolk Unit and both did their best to explain to them their own points of view concerning the circle's future. Hazel writes that 'it was a beautiful sunny day as we strolled across the sands. The circle was still covered by the sea and the destroyers didn't seem ready for us. I walked to the shoreline and asked the archaeologists to give their consent to enter the circle, advising them that I would be entering to do some work regardless; but with consent would leave after the work was done – they refused'. Nevertheless, Hazel and her companions entered the circle leaving the archaeologists with no option but to suspend work.

Crow's first visit to the site some days earlier also brought him face to face with the archaeologists and, though of a more confrontational nature than Hazel's visit, passed off just as peacefully. 'I asked them what their intentions were', writes Crow, 'they told me they intended to remove the oaks, I told them I intended to stop them; I went in and sat on the centre oak and meditated. Now, Norfolk Archaeology had put a circle of sandbags around the outer oaks to prevent sea and sand washing into their dig, so it came to me to remove the sand bags. . . so I threw the bags out. They tried to put them back so I threw them out and so on. They asked me to stop throwing out the sandbags', continues

Crow, 'I asked them to stop digging up the oaks, they started up their pump, I switched it off. I appealed to them to stop their work and to leave the oaks be, they called the police'.

With Crow countering every move made by the archaeologists, and the archaeologists doing much the same to Crow, the whole situation was rapidly descending into farce and matters didn't change with the arrival of the police. 'They asked me to leave the circle', writes Crow, 'I refused and they eventually went away. The archaeologists also went away as the tide started to come back in, washing around the oaks and eventually covering the circle'. With the tide rising around him Crow left the circle and retired further up the beach. The excavation had been all but halted that day and Crow fully intended to continue his peaceful protest at every available opportunity.

As far as the archaeologists were concerned they were simply trying to get on with their jobs and the presence of the protesters was simply one other difficult aspect on an already difficult site. However, barring one or two minor incidents, the protesters and the archaeologists both took the others presence in good spirits and throughout the early days of the excavation the general feeling around the circle was good humoured. As Hazel herself writes, 'After my first visit I did not have too many problems with the archaeologists that I dealt with'. With senior officials from both the Norfolk Archaeological Unit and English Heritage steering well clear of the controversial site until later in the excavation it was left to the on site supervisor, Mark Brennand, to deal with the day to day running of the dig. With the work falling behind schedule and protesters occupying the circle on a regular basis the situation could well have deteriorated. However, the archaeologists on the beach appear to have behaved, under the circumstances, in an exemplary manner and Mark Brennand's careful management kept a difficult situation from becoming a great deal worse.

The protesters were certainly slowing the efforts of the archaeologists to remove the timbers but, as they all realised, this would not be enough. Eventually, come what may, the archaeologists would succeed in their efforts. They had all the power of English Heritage behind them, the protesters had virtually no resources; all the archaeologists had to do was wait until it became impractical for the protesters to remain at the site day after day. If the protesters wanted to halt the excavation then they realised that they must halt it permanently and their only chance of doing that was through the courts.

On the 7 June the protesters, under the guidance of Buster Nolan, went to a firm of local solicitors to attempt to put a legal halt to the excavation. However, this action would have been impossible, due to the protesters' limited funds, had it not been for the aid and intervention of local businessman Mervyn Lambert and additional promises of financial support from the Council of British Druid Orders. Mr Lambert, who had already voiced his deep concern over the plight of the monument, committed himself to backing the protesters' fight and was shortly afterwards reported as saying that 'the battle has now begun. This isn't just hippies and druids. The ordinary people of Norfolk should make their voice heard to protect their heritage'.

Mervyn Lambert's views were supported and reiterated by Rollo Maughfling of the COBDO who felt that a legal answer was the only long term solution to the problem. 'If Buster is able to obtain some kind of legal measure', he is reported in the Eastern Daily Press as saying, 'we hope it will act as an interim holding order. It is extraordinary that this monument has come to light at all, and to bag it up and remove it without really understanding it is sacrilege. Nothing has been established about the wisdom of moving this artefact', he continued, 'which could prove very significant in the ancient spiritual geography of Britain. I really think this ought to come out in public debate'.

Unfortunately, the hopes of Buster and the other protesters for a legal end to the excavation was short lived. No firm of solicitors was willing to carry out an action against English Heritage and the Norfolk Archaeological Unit, believing that the sanctioning of the dig by the Board of Commissioners at English Heritage precluded any chance of a victory in the courts. After all, English Heritage would have been able to put themselves over as 'the' experts, draw on dozens of expert witnesses to support them and generally portray the protesters as the 'lunatic fringe'. Had the case ever reached the courts the solicitors believed that the chances of a high court judge deciding against a government organisation, and in favour of the druids, was limited in the extreme.

"Showdown at Seahenge"

With all chance of legally halting the excavation in the courts now gone the protesters once more returned to the tried and tested method of peaceful protest. By occupying the circle on set days, when excavations were due to take place, the protesters could limit the amount of work that the archaeologists could carry out. With a very limited 'window of opportunity' available to the archaeologists, due to the tides that covered the circle for most of each day, the peaceful occupation of the site began to put them seriously behind schedule. With the funds provided by English Heritage looking in danger of being exhausted before the work was anywhere near completion the Norfolk archaeologists decided to take a dramatic step; they would attempt to remove the central stump.

It appears that the senior archaeologists believed that by removing the central tree stump from the monument they would remove the focal point of the circle for the .protesters. Still bearing its wounds from the chainsaw the central stump had become a discussion point, a focus for debate and a painful reminder to the archaeologists of previous mistakes. With fourteen of the outer posts already gone they believed that if they could remove the central oak then the battle was as good as won. Feeling confident they scheduled the removal for Tuesday the 15 June.

Unfortunately, at least for the archaeologists, the plans for the lifting of the main trunk were known to a lot more people than they would have liked. Crow, still a regular protester at the site, writes 'the shout went out that they intended to remove the centre oak on the 15th. Men, women, children and a couple of dogs gathered in and around the oak circle. Norfolk Archaeology were there in their Landrovers with the police, English Heritage, council officials and the media. English Heritage asked us to leave the site', continues Crow, 'saying it was dangerous because of the deep holes they had dug to remove some of the oaks, the water was up to our knees and we couldn't see the ground, none of us fell down any of the holes'.

'We looked up the beach', Crow writes, 'and saw three diggers approaching, belching out roaring black smoke and chewing up the beach; tools of destruction that for years have been tearing up our lands, trees and now our sacred sites. We stood our ground inviting others to come in (to the circle). The diggers stopped about one hundred yards or so from the circle, we shouted to them to leave. We were asked to move away by the police, we refused'. Ensconced inside the circle, and with the archaeologists, police and digger drivers standing idly by, the protesters linked hands and began singing, chanting and playing music while the world's press looked on.

Hazel, the environmental protester from Cambridgeshire and on her first visit to the site, takes up the story. 'Eventually David Miles (Chief Archaeologist for English Heritage) enters the circle to speak to us. As he takes his first step I repeat the warnings given to us, and he slides into one of his own holes! A softly spoken man who informs us that he has only been on the project \ in the job for six weeks and if he had been there earlier no chainsaw would have been used. He disagreed with what had been done – but refused to admit this to the press. He told us that they would not be working that day', concludes Hazel, 'we said we'll stay until the heavy plant had gone'.

The senior archaeologists now realised that their plans for that day had gone badly awry and that it would be impossible to carry out any work with so many protesters occupying the circle. The local police were unwilling to attempt to remove the protesters, having been previously informed of their peaceful intentions, and English Heritage, under the glare of the media spotlights, had little option but to withdraw. 'The diggers moved away across the sand amid our cheers', writes Hazel, 'They looked like crabs – no, more like creatures with heads bowed in shame scuttling away to hide". She continues, "To enter and spend time in the circle is a great privilege ; my feelings are that it is more powerful than Stonehenge. Even with all the madness going on outside the circle I felt safe'.

The media response to the sit-in at Seahenge was mixed. Although many representatives from the national press and media services were present on the beach that day, ostensibly to watch the removal of the central oak, few of them reported on it in any detail. The tabloids, faced with only a peaceful protest and no heated confrontation, preferred to concentrate their efforts on the discovery in London of a Tudor banana. To the relief of English Heritage and many of the senior archaeologists the banana had a lot more media appeal, making the front page of certain tabloids, than their blighted efforts to overcome the protesters.

The local press, however, were quick to cover the story in some depth. The Eastern Daily Press, under the headline 'Showdown at Seahenge', gave prominence to the protesters small victory and referred to the days events as 'the battle of spiritualism against science'. Although reiterating the opinions of many people, that the delays caused by the protest were of little long term significance, the paper made a point of interviewing Buster Nolan, David Miles and others involved in the day's events. 'A day without a dig is great news', Buster is reported as saying, 'It means more people can come and see it before its gone. It demonstrates what a few small people can do against a national organisation. It shows English Heritage can't just assume it can come and take what it wants'. David Miles, on the other hand, was less willing to be drawn about the actions of the protesters and preferred to concentrate upon the disappointment of the archaeologists. 'We came with a lot of expectation', he was reported as saying, 'about what we might find under the stump. Because it was a ritual site of 2000 BC we have the possibility of finding food offerings, parts of weapons and human remains'.

It appears that the 'sit-in' at Seahenge was having the desired effect. A great number of the general public, already generally hostile to the idea of the circle's removal, found themselves drawn to the side of the protesters. The fight had taken on the form of a David and Goliath struggle between the government backed English Heritage and the little local people standing up for their beliefs; with the local archaeologists caught between the two. As ever, the sentimental traits of the British public led them to support the little people against the bigger 'bullies'. This swinging of support in the protesters favour was amply demonstrated at the time by a 'phone-in' debate hosted by BBC Radio Norfolk. The station, to its own surprise, received 7,689 calls of which 6,269 stated that the circle should not be moved. Only 1,420 callers expressed their support from the circles excavation and many more people complained afterwards that the time allowed for the 'phone-in' had been too short; they had been unable to get through on the busy lines.

Faced with such strong, and increasingly vocal, opposition English Heritage and the Norfolk Archaeology Unit once more bowed to public pressure. After all, they did not want to be cast in the role of villains and still believedthat they were pursuing the correct, and wisest, course of action. If the public were coming to understand the importance of the monument then all well and good; all they were trying to do was save it from being washed away by the sea. Reporting on the archaeologists change of heart the Eastern Daily Press quoted a spokesman for the Norfolk Archaeological Unit as saying that 'we want to move forward with general acceptance, if not total acceptance, that this is the right thing to do'.

In an attempt to resolve the situation, or at least find some sort of common ground with the protesters, English Heritage stated that they would stop all further work on the circle until a meeting could be convened between all sides of the debate. The majority of the protesters, taking the offer by English Heritage at face value, held off their protests until the meeting could be organised. The date was set for June the 22nd and the meeting was to be held at the Le Strange Arms Hotel in the neighbouring sea-side resort of Hunstanton.

However, the agreement by the archaeologists to cease all work until the meeting was convened was not honoured. A few days prior to the agreed date for the gathering Geoff Needham was disgusted to discover that certain archaeologists had returned to Holme Dunes in breach of the agreement. With no protesters present they had made the most of the opportunity and had removed two more of the outer posts of the circle. Geoff, like many other protesters who learnt of this complete disregard for their views, now felt that all mutual trust and respect between the two sides had evaporated. Despite their assurances, and outward signs of compromise and understanding, the archaeologists just could not be trusted. No longer able to have faith in any statements issued by the archaeologists Geoff felt that to attend any meeting with English Heritage and the Norfolk Archaeological Unit would be a complete waste of time. The relationship and dialogue, as far as he was concerned, had broken down irreparably.

The archaeologists involved in the incident had a very different story to tell, and one that was put out at the time and was all but ignored. The two posts that they had removed after the agreed halt to excavation were, they claimed, already prepared for lifting. Most of the clay and peat had already been removed from around their bases prior to the agreement being reached. Had they not returned to the site to finish the job they had started then the two posts in question stood a very good chance of being washed away on the next tide.

Midsummer Sunrise

However, the day before the meeting was scheduled to take place in Hunstanton the Druids and spiritualists gathered together at Holme Dunes to celebrate the midsummer solstice out at the circle. For the pagans among them the festival was one of the most important times of the year, marking as it did the high point in the yearly passage of the sun, a time of borders and transition, and they were determined to see the sun rise over the circle for one last time; before it was gone forever.

The night before the solstice sunrise, in the evening of the 20 June, Hazel, Crow and a few friends travelled to Holme to watch the night through on the beach. 'About six of us arrived at Holme Bay at about midnight', writes Crow, 'the tide was up so we couldn't see the oak circle. We marked a circle in the sand in line with Seahenge and performed a ritual. We took shelter near the dunes', he continues, 'began our vigil and awaited the solstice sunrise – the centre and turn of the year'. According to Hazel they spent 'a cold but peaceful night on the beach. We were hoping Sam (Jones) was going to make it – the beach was empty'.

Crow continues the story. *'As dawn approached, the sky getting lighter, we headed to our circle on the beach and as we did, from amongst the dunes along the beach, came many others, all emerging to greet the sun at this time and at this place, it was breathtaking. We moved into our circle and circles of people were forming along the beach – some standing alone yet we were all together'.* Hazel too was touched by this moment. *'The sun began to rise over the sea',* she writes, *'and we made our way back to the circle. Suddenly there were groups of people emerging from the dunes; there to pay respect in their own way and to watch the light of the shore. Beautiful'.*

There was no organised solstice celebration planned for the beach at Holme; no one gathered everyone together to be one the beach that morning and yet, as the sun rose over the sea, there were dozens of people there to greet it. All of them had decided to see in midsummer day at the circle for their own reasons.

Some had arrived alone, some in small groups, yet, as the first light struck the shore, they had all been joined together; joined by a special feeling of place and wonder at the true beauty of nature. With or without the circle Holme Bay is a special place.

Strange Meeting

Those taking part in the meeting gathered together the following afternoon at the Le Strange Arms Hotel in Hunstanton, a few miles from Holme. English Heritage were represented by Philip Walker and David Miles, who had been authorised to speak for the landowner, and Mark Brennand and Bill Boismier attended to represent the Norfolk Archaeological Unit. There were also two representatives of the Norfolk Wildlife Trust present, the occupiers of the site, to give an insight into the environmental aspects of the work being carried out. Sam Jones, Crow, Lauren Bleach and Linda Gerrigan represented the protesters while Shelley Waldrick was present in her role as a spokesperson for the local residents. The meeting was to be chaired by Clare Prout, a spiritualist who had actually campaigned for the circle's excavation when English Heritage had stated that they only wanted to record the site before leaving it to the sea.

It was also made known that the organisers of the meeting had invited Buster Nolan, Geoff Needham and Mervyn Lambert to attend but none of the three were present. Buster, living many miles away in Essex, had only been informed about the meeting the previous day and was unable to physically reach the venue. The same was true of Mr Lambert who, with a business to run, could not change his plans at such short notice. Besides this fact, Buster, like Geoff Needham, now felt that any discussion with the archaeologists and English Heritage was rather pointless. They had given their word that no further excavation would take place before the meeting was convened but had then gone ahead with the removal of two further timbers. In both Buster and Geoff's eyes English Heritage were not to be trusted. Why should any commitment given by them at this meeting be any less easy for them to ignore as and when it suited them?

The meeting did not get off to a terribly auspicious start. Clare Prout attempted to open the meeting by stating, what she believed were, the aims of the gathering. These three aims were, she believed, to be:-

● Share information and knowledge about all aspects of the site.
● Agree how the excavation might go ahead.
● Decide how the excavated timbers might be managed.

However, Crow immediately stated that he could not agree with the aims as set out by Clare Prout. He could not, under any circumstances, give his blessing to the removal of the timbers and, as far as he was concerned, they should not be talking about how the excavation might go ahead but rather if it should go ahead at all. This significant point was agreed as a starting point for the discussion. It was also agreed that a 'talking stick' would be used during the discussion. A talking stick, like the Indian talking feather, is passed around the members of the group. Only the person holding the stick is allowed to talk, thus eliminating any chances of the louder members of the group drowning out the less vocal.

The individuals were then asked to introduce themselves to the group and give a brief outline of their interests in the site. At this point Clare asked all the members of the group to hold hands and Crow was called upon to invite the presence of their ancestors and deities to help guide them in this matter. As a group the 'Awen', a Druidic chant, was sung.

The meeting lasted about five hours in total and many points were raised that both sides felt were both pertinent and important. David Miles, the chief archaeologist at English Heritage, once again stated that he was profoundly sorry that a chainsaw had been used on the central oak; but pointed out that this had taken place before he took up his post. Everyone agreed that this situation had been handled badly and that the press, rather than just reporting the story of the excavation and debate, seemed only interested in conflict. Furthermore, all those present stated their concern for the wildlife and birdlife of the beach and the effect that the increased visitor numbers were having upon it.

In total all those at the meeting agreed upon seven separate points which, to give a tenor of the meeting, it is probably worth giving here in full. The seven points of agreement were:-

● The site should be treated with respect.

● The site was sacred to the people who created it.

● It remains sacred to a large number of people today.

● The site contains a lot of information that can be shared, from archaeological to geomantic, and this should be shared.

● The beach is profoundly vulnerable.

● The current trend of visitor numbers will irrevocably damage the site.

● That the damage done by the visitors will result in the death of birds by starvation and exhaustion, and of the decline in their numbers because they will be unable to feed.

The minutes of the meeting, which have been posted on the 'Time Team' web site and in various other places, then go on to list six conclusions that it states were also agreed by all the members. These conclusions, as read, give the impression that it was agreed that the excavation should go ahead on or after the 28 June and that the timbers should then go to Flag Fen for conservation. However, Sam Jones, Crow and the other protesters do not agree with this version of events. Neither Sam or Crow, at any point, agreed that the excavation should continue.

Writing after the event Crow himself gave a concise, and to the point, summary of what he believed had actually taken place. 'Everyone there had a chance to talk and listen', he writes, 'to all view points present and there was some good ground covered with English Heritage saying they would act differently in the future. I heard Norfolk Archaeology's, English Heritage's and English Nature's viewpoints even though I did not agree with them all. I said that I felt that Seahenge should remain and those pieces removed should be replaced. Unfortunately, English Heritage and Norfolk Archaeology said they fully intended to remove Seahenge and it was suggested that if this happened another should be put in its place. I stated that I could not give my blessings to any part of Seahenge being removed. Unfortunately', concludes Crow, 'the outcome of that meeting has been distorted by a number of sources including English Heritage reports (and) a report on the *Time Team* web site'.

According to several of those present at the meeting, Crow's view, that no agreement was reached concerning excavation, is correct. The later reports, that were issued from several sources, made it appear that agreements had been reached concerning the circle's future were, at best. misleading and, at worst a fabrication. Crow, Sam Jones, Hazel, Buster and their friends vowed to continue their battle to save the oak circle.

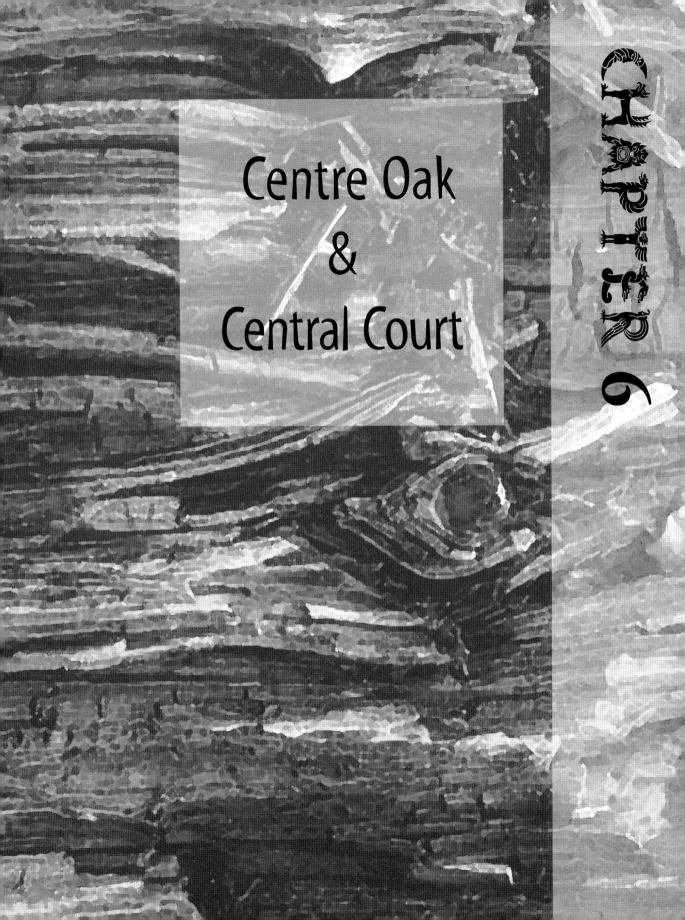

Centre Oak
&
Central Court

CHAPTER 6

The excavation of the circle at Holme Dunes was scheduled to restart on Monday the 28 June. However, almost as soon as preparations were made to continue with the dig it looked likely that work would once again have to be suspended. English Heritage, since the 'sit-in' earlier in the month, had now taken the view that if there was any threat of disruption from protesters no work would be carried out. The situation would be reviewed upon a daily basis and only when the coast was, quite literally, clear would they continue to lift the timbers.

The day before work was due to restart the local police force received word that some sort of protest was to take place on the beach the following day. Amid rumours that extra protesters had been recruited from among the ranks of those who had clashed with police at Stonehenge the previous week it seemed likely that the protests, rather than diminishing in size, would actually grow. In a report published in the Eastern Daily Press Police Sergeant Joe Callaghan, based at Hunstanton, stated that he did not know how many protesters were en route to the site or the type of groups that would be represented. 'We're not sending anyone down to keep people away. We're non confrontational and we'll react to whatever comes along. Everyone's talking to each other but everyone's disagreeing'.

The article then went on to interview Philip Shalicross, joint chief of the British Druid Order, who was quick to point out that the people who caused trouble at Stonehenge had no connection with the Druid orders. 'They come from a variety of places', he was reported as saying, 'but weren't interested in the summer solstice, spiritualism or druidry. It would be a shame if people determined on confrontation turn up at Holme to cause trouble'.

As it transpired, the hordes of new age travellers expected to arrive at the site to cause mayhem never appeared. Instead the only protesters at the circle were Buster Nolan, Crow and three others who enjoyed a 'peaceful protest picnic' in the summer sunshine on the near deserted beach. The archaeologists, however, stayed away and the protesters' only visitors that day were a film crew from Yorkshire Television and Pat Fisher who was carrying out an on-going recording programme for her web site (www.northcoastal.freeserve.co.uk).

As the last days of June went by it appeared likely that the archaeologists would soon be able to remove the central oak and the rest of the outer circle. The protesters that were able to make it to the site each day were too few in number to be able to halt the excavation outright and even they were beginning to feel the strain. 'I got harsh to deal with at times', writes Crow, 'witnessing the oaks being dug around, the carnage, the greed of the archaeologists, the destruction. At times I felt physically sick'. For Buster Nolan too, who had been involved since the first news of the circle had come to light via Sam Jones, the whole situation was getting difficult. He had made the long trip up from Essex on countless occasions and even his patience and stamina were becoming strained.

Rollo Maughfling, the Archdruid of Stonehenge and Glastonbury, soon began to realise that the Holme protesters needed some extra support. 'On the 30 June I received a call from Buster', writes Rollo, 'who sounded like a man close to tears. "This beautiful tree circle", he said "it's been here for four thousand years, and now that its visible again, for everyone to enjoy, all they want to do is destroy it". He asked me for help. That night I resolved to go up to Norfolk the next day and see what I could do. It seemed to me that by now the urgency of the situation called for an official Druidic Proclamation'.

Then in the early hours of the following morning Rollo Maughfling left his home in the peaceful Vale of Avalon in Somerset and made the long journey by car to Norfolk. He had arranged to meet Buster and fellow protester Simon in the neighbouring town of Hunstanton early in the morning to catch the low tide at Holme. 'It was a grey, wet day, with everything seawards looking stormy and menacing as we covered the last few miles', writes Rollo, 'Surprise, surprise, we had an escort for the last leg of the journey from the local constabulary, a sergeant and a constable who knew Buster and were well aware of his continued efforts to keep the protest within the law. Knowing that I was scheduled to perform an official druidic proclamation at the site, we duly informed the police of our intentions, who thanked us for keeping them informed, and promptly drove off again'.

Buster, Simon and Rollo were not the only protesters to be making their way down to the beach that morning. Crow, who had been keeping vigil at the site for the previous weeks, was also making his customary half mile trek out to the circle 'with staff in hand and in the distance I could see three robed figures (Buster, Rollo and Simon) with staffs approaching from the other end of the beach. Then I noticed on the beach, near where the oaks would soon emerge, the biggest blackest bird I had ever seen; which I wasn't sure was a bird at all. Then the bird took off, circled over the sea where the oaks were soon to emerge, then disappeared into the waves'. The bird, if that was what it was, was not seen by the other three who quickly came to join Crow.

'After meeting Crow, the only resident protester', writes Rollo, 'we decided to head off across the beach to the shoreline, to see what the retreating tide would reveal. By now it was a beautiful sunny afternoon (to Rollo, who had been awake since the early hours, it merely seemed like afternoon. It was, in fact, still late morning) on a completely deserted golden beach that seemed to stretch on forever. Just us, the sand, the sea and the birds. Then Buster grabbed my arm. 'Look, there it is' he said. And sure enough there were the first of the remaining and by now familiar weathered looking wooden posts emerging from the waves'. As we watched', continues Rollo, 'up popped another, and another, and then, all at once, the magnificent upturned central tree formation, sea water pouring off it and lapping round it. A shiver ran down my spine as I realised that the sea was revealing something most of us have only read about in books'.

A Druid Proclamation

This was Rollo Maughfling's first visit to the site and, like many others before him, he was deeply affected by the circle's emergence from the sea. However, the tranquil calm that the protesters had first experienced arriving at the beach that morning was not going to last for long. 'Suddenly there was a noise and a commotion behind us', writes Rollo, 'Norfolk Archaeology Unit Landrovers were shattering the peace and quiet by heading towards us at full tilt. They screeched to a halt and out came ropes and stakes and spades and buckets and pumps and compressors and all the paraphernalia of the removal business. Behind them, blue light flashing, came a police patrol car with senior officers on board. Behind them came T.V crews and reporters and the whole sea-side circus of on-the-spot media coverage. And behind them, on foot, local people wanting to see the treasure for themselves'.

'As the sea retreated further', continues Rollo, ' and archaeologists in green wellies headed out into the waves with ropes and stakes in order to cordon off the whole area, I realised it was now or never. I announced that I had an official druidic proclamation to make and that I would be doing so, stood barefoot, on the central oak. The leading archaeologist appealed to the police to prevent me from doing so. I explained that under our common law rights of religious assembly granted by King Richard I in 1189, we had every right to do so'. The police, carrying out a policy of non-intervention, a policy they upheld throughout the series of protests on the beach, allowed Rollo to continue.

With no one now trying to stop him Rollo Maughfling, Archdruid of Stonehenge and Glastonbury, 'waded out into the sea and climbed up onto the central altar of the Seahenge oak timbered circle, and began to make our druidic proclamation to the assembled crowd of onlookers, well-wishers and others. But not without first having to find my balance. And in that split second, between finding my balance and my voice, and nearly losing both, I suddenly remembered that old schooldays tale of King Canute, and felt how he must have felt, trying to make the waves go back, in the vain attempt to prove to the world that you cannot legislate against Nature'.

The proclamation read out by Rollo from the central oak was simple and to the point. In its eight articles it listed the reasons why the circle should not be removed and stated that the circle was a national monument and not a museum piece. It further went on to point out that the circle was site specific and of religious importance to many thousands of people; to remove it would be like trying to move Stonehenge or Canterbury Cathedral. The proclamation called on the archaeologists to preserve the circle *in situ* whilst further researches into its origins and purpose were carried out.

However, things had gone too far. No simple Druid proclamation, no matter how well meaning, and no handful of protesters could halt the excavation. With the protesters cleared from the circle the archaeologists once more resumed their task. 'Later', writes Rollo, 'we watched the depressing spectacle of the licensed exhumation carrying on unabated, as though nothing had happened. Mud everywhere. Protesters and local people remonstrating with students and archaeologists alike. Archaeologists ignoring everything'. Everyone was by now tired and upset. The atmosphere around the circle was strained as described by Rollo. 'I was tired. Everything seemed a blur. Buster was explaining to everyone why it wasn't right to break up ancient sacred sites for the museum and tourist industry, he looked over at the young student diggers and said 'Would you still be doing this job if they told you to dig up Stonehenge?'

At which point one of the senior archaeologists lost his rag. He came up behind Buster poking him with his finger and telling him to leave them alone. Buster wisely retreated; having spent weeks ensuring that the protest was peaceful and that no violence ensued'.

This unfortunate incident, the only one of its kind during the entire protest, put a blight upon the whole day. Everyone involved felt that it was uncalled for. After the whispering campaigns of the previous weeks, when it had been suggested that the protesters were likely to emulate the violent incidents seen at Stonehenge that midsummer, it was ironic that it was an archaeologist who finally lost his temper.

The protesters left the site that afternoon with heavy hearts. They had carried on their campaign of peaceful protest for many weeks and yet, despite the support they were receiving locally, their efforts were seemingly in vain. At every low tide the archaeologists came back to remove yet more timbers and it appeared to be only a matter of time before the entire circle was gone. Rollo Maughfling made his way back to Somerset while the others, Buster, Simon and Crow, vowed to continue with the protest for as long as was practical. Unfortunately, this was not to be.

A Legal Injunction

Unbeknownst to the protesters English Heritage had decided to try and end all the protests surrounding the site once and for all. The day following Rollo's proclamation at the oak circle (Friday, July 2nd) they managed to obtain an interim injunction that specifically forbade the protesters from going to the site. The injunction named Rollo Maughfling, Buster Nolan, Geoff Needham, Des Crow and 'John Doe', and threatened them with arrest and criminal proceedings if they tried to interfere with the archaeologists work. The final name on the injunction, John Doe, rather than being a specific person, was a 'cover-all' name that referred to anyone else who might seek to occupy the site. In effect, English Heritage had taken out an injunction against every member of the British population and now had the legal right to ban anyone they wished from approaching the circle.

However, although caught by surprise by the legal injunction the protesters were not simply going to lie down and give up. That weekend local businessman, Mervyn Lambert, spent several thousand pounds at the Norfolk County Court trying to defend those named in the injunction. The protesters, it was pointed out, had not even been served with a notice of proceedings, although their addresses were well known to English Heritage. They had no opportunity to defend themselves or to put their side of the argument and, as the site was not a scheduled monument, English Heritage had no overriding legal right to ban them from the site. The court was sympathetic to Mr Lambert and the proceedings were adjourned until the following Tuesday (July 6th) when it would be heard in the High Courts of Justice in London when everyone would have a chance to put their own case.

The injunction against Geoff Needham, the local parish councillor, was seen by many as particularly heavy handed. Geoff was a protester to the excavation, of that there wasno doubt, but he had simply tried to publicise the plight of the monument. At no time had Geoff occupied the circle to prevent work being carried out and it seemed that the authorities were simply trying to make an example of him. 'I have to go down to defend my name', Geoff is reported as saying, 'I am a Common Right Holder and am entitled to be on the beach going about my lawful business. I have not obstructed the 'dig'. I have been filming the whole business, but that hardly constitutes obstruction'. And so, on the morning of the 2 July, Geoff, Rollo, Buster and Crow found themselves at the Royal High Courts of Justice in London preparing to defend their actions.

The protesters had little time to prepare themselves and upon arrival at the court were handed a 'massive file' full of legal papers that constituted the case against them. Due to the sudden nature of the hearing, and the prohibitive cost involved, none of the protesters had employed the services of a barrister; preferring instead to defend themselves. The hearing lasted an entire day and for the protesters it was a day well spent. 'The first judge who was about to hear the case stood down', writes Rollo, 'because he was a member of English Heritage. Thus we ended up instead in front of Mrs Justice Arden, who was keen to hear the arguments for both sides. The barrister for English Heritage presented their case, complete with photographs of everything that occurred at Seahenge the previous Wednesday (the day of Rollo's visit). Then it was our turn to defend ourselves'.

The protesters then put their arguments to the judge, stressing that they had only sought to preserve the site from the inappropriate actions of the archaeologists. Geoff Needham, who had already pointed out that all he had sought to do was bring publicity to the plight of the circle, then went on to state that as a Common Right Holder he was as entitled as the archaeologists, if not more so, to be on the beach where the circle was found as it was 'Common' land. Geoff Needham had, perhaps without really realising its true significance, stumbled upon the one legal area in which English Heritage could, in the right circumstances, be bested. The issues surrounding 'Rights of Common' are complex in the extreme but, because of the bearing they may have on the overall debate, are worth mentioning in some detail.

'Along the coast of North Norfolk there are extensive marshlands between the dunes running alongside the sea and higher ground. The marshes and dunes have provided sustenance to the villagers of the coastal regions since their formation and over the years villagers established their rights to this provision. The land, therefore, became known as 'Common' and the villagers the 'Common Right Holders'. Every villager knew that through long standing custom he or she had a right to freely use the marsh produce until, in 1965, there came the Commons Registration Act. It then became necessary for every Common to be registered as such and every Commoner to register his rights over it. Proof had to be given that the land had been used as a Common and again proof provided of the existence of the rights that were being claimed and that a person had established his or her right to use them' - extract from the web site of the Scolt Head and District Common Right Holders Association.

Those people that are registered as Common Right Holders have an indisputable legal right to many items available on the Common, which in the case of coastal areas normally appears to extend right down to the low tide mark. The Rights of Common give the registered holders the right to take such items as seaweed, shellfish, wildfowl, game, sand, shingle, fish and also to graze their sheep, cattle, horses and geese upon the land. More relevant to the Seahenge debate, among the list of items that the right holders can collect is mentioned the term 'estovers'. This ancient term is usually defined as the right to collect any old and ancient timbers that may be discovered or washed up on the Common; to be used for buildings, repairs or as fuel.

The land upon which the timber circle was discovered was, without doubt, registered as 'Common' and Geoff Needham was a registered 'Common Right Holder'. In fact, Geoff was one of the first locals to register his rights, back in 1967, and was allocated 'Right Number One' for the area on the 23 June that year. Furthermore, due to the shared nature of the Common land between Holme and the neighbouring village of Thornham, there are 184 Common Right Holders registered as having rights over the area of land upon which Seahenge was discovered.

The legal implications of this are complex and, at times, confusing. In its most limited form it meant that English Heritage could not, without a major and far reaching legal battle, exclude Geoff from visiting what was, in effect, his own common land. To do so would have been an infringement of his rights as a Common Right Holder and any such action is likely to have encountered strong opposition from the Common Right Holders Associations that scatter Britain. The associations are justifiably jealous of their rights and the exclusion of a Common Right Holder from his own Common land would have set a dangerous precedent; a precedent that no association could allow to take place.

Secondly, and more importantly, as a Common Right Holder Geoff and one hundred and eighty three other local people actually had certain legal rights over any 'estovers' (old timbers) found on the Common land. The Seahenge timbers, if not legally declared to be a national monument, would be classified as 'estovers'. The removal of items that the Common Right Holders actually had rights to from the Common, even with the landowners permission, is a decidedly grey area. In more clear cut circumstances such a removal, without the consent of the Common Right Holders, could precipitate legal action being taken. However, this area of law is decidedly murky, relying, as it does, on cases of legal precedent stretching back many centuries, and the true legal position of both the Common Right Holders and English Heritage remain unclear. The 'Law of Commons' stretches back many centuries whereas English Heritage was only established in the 1980s; giving the Common Right Holders a decided advantage. In all likelihood the only true test of each parties position would come from a complex, and expensive, court case.

As it was, that day in the High Courts of Justice, English Heritage did not pursue the case against Geoff Needham, he having no case to answer, and the judge, Mrs Justice Arden, ruled that Geoff was to be excused from the injunction. Similarly the injunction against Rollo Maughfling was also deemed inappropriate, he having simply attempted to bring publicity to the issue, and both men were acquitted and awarded costs against English Heritage. The other three named in the injunctions, Des Crow, Buster Nolan and 'John Doe', were found to have a case to answer and all three had the injunction upheld against them. In effect, Buster, Crow and no other member of the British public would, in future, be allowed to interfere with the excavation works being carried out at Holme Dunes.

However, although Mrs Justice Arden did find in favour of English Heritage in these three cases she was not happy with the way they had acted throughout the whole affair. In her summing up, after quoting the Druidic Proclamation in full, she ruled that although she had no statutory power to halt the excavation she felt that English Heritage had not handled the affair well. 'Their actions have been perceived as provocative by a number of people', she stated, and, 'to an extent the problems have been brought to a head by, for instance, removing the slice from the oak which is the central bole in the tree circle. It was a large piece of wood and is very visible. Secondly, there has been, I understand from Mr Needham, no local meeting, and thirdly, this is a religious place of worship for the Druids and thus work done at the site has led to high feelings about the work being done. In those circumstances, to an extent, it seems to me that the claimant (English Heritage) must have brought this situation to a head by its own actions'.

Mrs Justice Arden then went on to rule that not only should English Heritage give a full account of its actions with regard to the use of a chainsaw on the central oak, but in future they should take into account the need for public consultation, especially on a local level, and respect the feelings and wishes of genuine religious groups such as those represented by the Council of British Druid Orders. She further stated that English Heritage should investigate the possibility of preserving the site further inland or, at the very least, give active consideration to the construction of a replica.

The ruling given by Mrs Justice Arden was, in the short term, a victory for English Heritage. The judge had upheld three of the five injunctions, including

that issued against 'John Doe' (or rather Joe Public), and it now appeared that nothing could stop the final excavations being carried out at Holme Dunes. However, in her summing up Mrs Justice Arden had been highly critical of the approach adopted by English Heritage and her recommendations for the future handling of similar situations may well be seen as something of a long term victory for the protesters. In future English Heritage should involve themselves in a process of public consultation, listening to and taking into account the views of the local people, and they should also respect the wishes of religious groups that have an interest in any future sites. They had, in fact, been given a sharp rap on the knuckles and told to do better next time.

Work Resumed

In the days following the court hearing it became apparent that English Heritage and the Norfolk Archaeological Unit were going to quickly follow up their victory by removing the remaining timbers as quickly as possible. With Buster Nolan and Crow, two of the most determined protesters, now banned from the site the archaeologists planned a hasty lifting of the remaining outer posts and the central oak stump. However, the work on the circle was still dictated by the tides and it was not until the 9th and 10th of July, four days after the hearing in London, that work was able to continue.

The weekend of the 10th and 11th saw the removal of several more of the timbers from the outer circle and on the Monday (12th) two more were lifted; leaving only about nine or ten still in position. The weekend was a quiet one on the beach, there being no protesters present, and the archaeologists had little more than a handful of journalists and a few hundred members of the public to contend with. When the weather and tides permitted the work continued and the number of timbers on the beach gradually dwindled as they were removed to Flag Fen. Finally, with the circle almost gone, English Heritage decided the time had come to remove the central oak. The root was prepared for lifting, having been excavated on all

sides and the date for removal was set; the main timber would be lifted on Friday the 16 July.

The morning of the 16th saw Holme beach become the scene of determined activity as final preparations were made to lift the main oak. News of the operation had leaked out and the area around the monument was filled with camera crews, journalists and press photographers, as well as several hundred members of the public. Amongst the crowd, unbeknownst to the archaeologists, were a number of protesters who, as equipment was brought on to the site and despite the court injunction, soon made their presence known. Although having very little chance of halting the final removal the protesters were determined to voice their opposition to the 'vandalism' that they believed was being carried out in the name of historical research.

As the day progressed diggers were moved up to the monument to be used in the final lifting operation and many senior archaeologists were on hand to supervise its removal. There had been much speculation as to what would be discovered beneath the centre oak, some suggesting that it may conceal sacrificial items, food or even human remains, and they believed that the time would soon be upon them when they would finally learn the truth. The chainsawed slice had been replaced with wooden wedges, to stabilise the structure, and the oak itself looked rather odd, having been swathed in thick bandage like cords designed to keep the wedges in place. The slings that had been wrapped around the oak were checked, the final deposits of sand were cleared from around its base and, with members of the crowd heckling the archaeologists, the diggers were moved into their lifting positions. Then, just when it seemed that the end of the excavation was in sight, the archaeologists hit one more snag.

Mervyn Lambert, the local businessman who had funded much of the opposition to the circles removal, was on hand to watch the last act in what he believed was a great tragedy unfolding itself on the beach. As a the owner of a large plant hire business he had seen many similar operations carried out and was not at all impressed with what was happening before him under the archaeologists direction. In his opinion the machine that the archaeologists were intending to use for the final lift was far too small to carry out the task effectively and safely. Using his mobile phone Mr Lambert immediately contacted the Health and Safety Executive and informed them of his opinions concerning the proposed lifting. Faced with a possible infringement of the health and safety guidelines the archaeologists asked the machinery operators if they were willing to continue using the machines that they had on site or if they would prefer to postpone the operations until a large vehicle had been secured. The plant operators, unsure of their legal position, decided to bring in a heavier machine just to be absolutely certain that they did not infringe the health and safety guidelines. However, the finding and collection of a larger machine would take several hours, by which time the tidal 'window of opportunity' would have passed. The oak would have to remain in place until the following day.

The following day (July 17th) the archaeologists were back on the beach. Mervyn Lambert's call to the Health and Safety Executive had not managed to halt the excavation of the central oak; merely given it a twenty four hour reprieve. Now, with a more suitable machine in place the final lift was to go ahead as planned. The new machine was positioned next to the oak and the lifting slings were attached to it. With archaeologists, locals, protesters and the press looking on the slack was taken up and the lifting began. The machine roared, the oak shuddered, and gradually the central oak of the timber circle began to rise.

The final lift took no more than a few minutes at most but to those who stood gazing at the four thousand year old oak as it rose slowly in the air it seemed much longer. Inch by inch it was prised from its ancient resting place until, finally, it swung free from the hole. Much to the surprise of the gathered locals and the press the bottom of the oak, rather than being a sharpened point, was cut into a flat base. With guide ropes attached to the stump the digger slowly reversed out of the circle with its precious burden swinging slowly in its slings. After four thousand years in Holme its next stop was to be Flag Fen.

As soon as the oak was removed the archaeologists were quick to probe the mysteries of the hole that it had once rested in. They hoped to find items that had been placed under the oak by the monument's original builders and anticipated a few surprises. At other monuments excavated in Britain it was not unusual to find a human sacrifice of some sort actually built into the structure. At both Avebury and the Sanctuary in Wiltshire sacrificial burials had been discovered in the past and it was anticipated that the central oak might have hidden many mysteries. At the very least they hoped to find sacrificial offerings such as food, pottery or even weapons; as it was the archaeologists were disappointed, the hole was empty. After two days further investigation into the hole all the archaeologists discovered was a fragment of the honeysuckle rope, lodged in the silts at the side of the hole, and a single hazelnut shell. At the request of local spiritualists an offering of branches and flowers was laid in the hole from which the oak had been removed and the area was back filled with silt.

Flag Fen

Later that day the oak trunk was transported out of Norfolk to join the rest of the excavated timbers at Flag Fen in Cambridgeshire. The few remaining timbers from the outer circle were later lifted and followed their fellows. Here, at the leading ancient timber preservation centre in Britain, the timbers were cleaned and stored in tanks of fresh running water. Then, and only then could Maisy Taylor, one of the site's archaeological directors and ancient timber specialist, study the timbers.

What was immediately apparent was that the timbers were in a remarkable state of preservation. The original tool marks, made by the site's builders some four thousand years previously, were clearly visible and it was possible to match up the markings with known tools of the period. This wonderful preservation, it is believed, was a side effect of the timbers having remained wet and in an oxygen free environment for so many centuries. If the timbers were to remain intact until full conservation work was carried out it was essential that they remained immersed in water. However, it also soon became obvious to Maisy that the timbers' relatively recent re-emergence had caused this process of natural preservation to begin to be reversed.

The cell structure of timbers that have been subjected to various levels of damp and differing temperature levels will, gradually over time, begin to break down. Over four thousand years this process has become very apparent in the Seahenge timbers and the only thing helping the timbers cells to retain their shape is the high concentration of mineral salts found in the wood. However, to preserve the timbers for any length of time these salts must be removed and by doing so the cells that make up the timbers will lose their structure. The only answer to this is, as the salts are removed, they must be replaced with something that support the cell structure and not attack the timbers.

This is now what is beginning to happen to the Seahenge timbers. The wood is constantly subjected to a spray of fresh water that will, over a number of years, remove the mineral salts. At one and the same time the water carries with it a water soluble wax that will replace the salts and stabilise the cellular structure of the wood. As the salts being washed out gradually diminish the concentration of wax is increased until, finally, the timbers will be thoroughly impregnated with the wax and once again stabilised. This process is much the same as that carried out on the Mary Rose, the Tudor warship lifted from the Solent, and is both time consuming and expensive.

To further complicate matters, Maisy Taylor also discovered that many of the timbers appeared to be rotting from the inside out. This strange phenomena was caused, she believed, by the infestation of a marine animal known commonly as a 'piddock' (pholas dactylus). These bi-valve molluscs, also known as 'ship-worms', quickly bore into any soft materials, such as timber, peat and chalk, and eat away at the timber from within. In the days of timber hulled ships these little animals, most especially its larger American cousin, caused untold damage. If not destroyed the molluscs will quickly spread throughout the whole timber and reduce it to a soaking and rotting honeycomb. In the case of the Seahenge timbers, most especially the central oak, these little animals have already bored between 18 and 20 inches into the wood. It is also interesting to note that these 'piddocks' are actually edible – although they leave you with a luminous mouth.

Where Next?

At the present time (April 2000) the Seahenge timbers are still undergoing study at Flag Fen in Cambridgeshire where they are on display to the public. In March of this year it was announced by English Heritage that the timbers will be returning to Norfolk in September of 2000. They will then be housed at the Rural Life Museum at Gressenhall, near Dereham, whilst conservation work is carried out. The work is to be undertaken by Norfolk Museums Service and paid for by English Heritage and is expected to take about two years for the smaller timbers and between three and five years for the central oak stump.

Once conservation work is complete the timber circle will be put on display somewhere in Norfolk, the exact location of which is, at the present time, yet to be decided. As canbe imagined the local views upon where the timbers should finally come to rest are strong indeed. John Lorimer speaks for many when he wrote 'it would surely be preferable for the timbers to be displayed and housed somewhere locally – yet, as the museum pointed out, funding would be a major issue. This would be a very popular move in the local community indeed. A museum \ archive, if one were to be established, perhaps with lottery money, and with Seahenge as its centrepiece, would provide an excellent magnet for local archaeology, and a source of much needed tourist revenue. . . It is certain such a museum would be a welcome addition'.

For Geoff Needham and Stephanie Middleton the idea of returning the timbers to the Holme area is really the only acceptable answer. 'They should be returned to Holme', writes Stephanie, 'with government or English Heritage funding. They were happy to spend a fortune removing the timbers from their home, now they should be prepared to bring them back'. Geoff Needham is of much the same opinion. 'English Heritage funded the removal', he writes, 'therefore they have, in my opinion, an obligation to see that the future of the circle is safeguarded – and that must mean funding by English Heritage. English Heritage gave an undertaking to the court that they would be returned to North Norfolk, preferably Holme – in which they belong'.

Of those who actually spent many hours on the beach at Holme Dunes trying to prevent the circle's removal there is really only one opinion. Crow, Hazel, Sam Jones and Rollo Maughfling would all like to see the circle returned to the Holme area. Rollo really speaks for all of them when he writes 'In our view, as with all ancient sites that have suffered erosion, Seahenge should be replaced some little distance inland on the same major axis of orientation as it originally was'.

However, as pointed out by John Lorimer, the final decision will probably be decided not by the local people, or even by the archaeologists, but by the accountants. Norfolk Museums Service has been facing budget problems for years and it is unlikely that things are going to massively improve in the near future. A new museum and display facility in the Holme area would cost many thousands of pounds; money that the museum service does not have and English Heritage is not likely to produce. It seems that all the uncertainty over the last few years concerning the circles future is set to continue. It appears that the fate of the circle is, once again, in the hands of the gods.

Time
Team
Trauma

CHAPTER 7

Just as everyone involved in the excavation and subsequent protest at Holme Dunes began to think that the debate was beginning to subside a fresh view of the proceedings came to the public's attention and interest in the circle was once more revived. On the 29 December 1999 Channel Four screened their *Time Team* Christmas special. The programme, which covered the debate, excavation and subsequent reconstruction of the Holme timber circle, suddenly brought all the old issues rising to the surface once more; and even raised a few new ones of its own. As the *Time Team* website itself proudly proclaims 'Never before has a Time Team programme been the focus of so much public interest and controversy'.

Time Team, for those who have not found themselves rushing home early on Sunday afternoons, is a series of hour long Channel Four television productions that investigate archaeological sites. Fronted by Tony Robinson, the programme deals with a new site each episode, investigating and excavating each one over a period of only three days. With a team of archaeologists, scientists, artists, computer graphic specialists and historians the aim is to learn as much about each site as possible in the time allowed and present the results to the public as and when they occur.

The series has been highly successful in the past, having excavated in North America, Mallorca and Northern Ireland, as well as on a multitude of British sites, and has been instrumental in bringing to light many important, and previously unknown, archaeological sites. The teams most spectacular discovery (although every viewer appears to have their own favourite) was probably that made at Tockenham in Wiltshire where they managed to locate a previously unknown Roman villa. The villa, it later transpired, had been almost completely removed; the stone having been re-used nearby, but *Time Team's* geophysical survey managed to map out the entire complex; a complex that had been unknown even a week earlier. It was later discovered that the villa had once possessed a large mosaic floor; had it survived it would have been the third largest such structure ever found in Britain.

Discoveries such as the Roman villa at Tockenham have made *Time Team* one of the most popular television programmes about archaeology ever screened. It has led to archaeology being understood by a much wider audience and has gone a long way towards demystifying the whole field of physical archaeology. In its early programmes the team were commonly investigating sites proposed by the general public but as the programme has received greater support from the archaeological community they are increasingly asked by local archaeologists to assist in the investigation of known sites. 'Time Team' have made several visits to Norfolk prior to their involvement in the Seahenge project and at sites such as Bawsey, the subject of a 'Time Team Live' programme, they have worked in close conjunction with the Norfolk Archaeological Unit.

However, as 'Time Team' themselves are keen to stress, the Seahenge Christmas Special was no ordinary 'Time Team' programme. The team itself was to have no part in the actual excavation itself, nor did they have any input into the decision to excavate. Rather, the programme was to simply record the excavation as it progressed, follow the associated research and attempt to present the findings to the public. The main area of their involvement, and an area in which they have made considerable advances in the past, was in field of 'experimental archaeology'.

These days the term 'experimental archaeology' is usually used to cover such activities as building reconstructions, the use of original building methods, original tools and, where possible, original materials. The idea behind experimental archaeology is that by recreating as closely as possible the original structure or site, archaeologists will be able to better understand the remains they discover during excavation. It is also hoped that such practices will enable all those involved to gain a better understanding of the actual people whom they are studying, the problems they faced and the methods used to overcome them. Although frowned upon by serious archaeologists for many years the practical side of experimental archaeology is now undergoing a widespread revival.

In fact, in recent years experimental archaeology has had one or two notable successes that have led the archaeological community to dramatically re-think their views. For example the recreation of the longbows found aboard the Tudor warship the Mary Rose have brought to light many previously unknown aspects of Tudor military archery, and the erection of several replica stones from Stonehenge, using only a bare two hundred people, has caused historians to rethink the idea that the structure needed the labour of many thousands to build. At the time of writing a small team of enthusiasts are engaged in a experiment to drag a 'bluestone' from the mountains of Wales to the site of Stonehenge in Wiltshire; just to prove that it can be done using the technology of the time. Such enlightening experiments are merely the tip of the iceberg and experimental archaeology, as practised by such groups as *Time Team,* has become a respected field or research.

For the *Time Team Christmas Special* experimental archaeology was to play an important part. The team hoped, with the aid of acknowledged timber and metallurgy experts, to be able to reconstruct the circle to show how it might well have looked when first built. They were aiming to use both original materials, techniques and replicas of the original tools in their efforts to learn more about the monument's builders. However, before any of this could begin they first had to record the actual excavation and, inevitably, much of the debate that surrounded it.

When the agreement was reached between the makers of *Time Team* and the authorities involved in the project at Holme Dunes it was made clear, as a condition of filming, that none of the actual team themselves were to be present on site. Mindful of the already growing debate the local archaeologists and English Heritage did not want to leave themselves open to any further criticism and would only allow Graham Johnson, one of the *Time Team* cameramen, access to the area. All other *Time Team* personnel, including Tony Robinson, the presenter, and Mick Aston, the teams chief archaeologist, would have to keep a specified distance from where the actual work was taking place.

In the circumstances this decision, forestalling, as it did, any accusations of flippancy on the part of the archaeologists, may have been a wise one, but for those directly effected by it, in particular Mick Aston, it must have appeared harsh. Mick Aston, as well as being the archaeological

team leader for *Time Team,* is also the current Professor of Landscape Archaeology at the University of Bristol and has written many articles and books upon the subject. An acknowledged expert in his field Mick has appeared in no less than six series on archaeology for Channel Four alone and has been working as an archaeologist for over thirty years. During the mid 1970's Mick served as county archaeologist for Somerset and gained extensive experience of ancient timbers while studying the finds, such as the 'Sweet track', that were emerging from the area known as the Somerset levels.

This track-way, built nearly six thousand years ago and consisting of a single line of wooden planks stretching for almost two kilometres, was used by the prehistoric inhabitants of the area to traverse the sodden marshland. Named after the peat digger who first uncovered it, the 'Sweet track' represents one of the oldest man made structures yet discovered in Europe. In many respects the timbers emerging from the peat at Holme were extremely similar in nature to those discovered on the Somerset levels. For Mick Aston to be excluded from the site of the excavation, bearing in mind that any member of the public could walk all over the site if they so wished, must have appeared as a trifle unfair.

Whereas 'Time Teams' involvement with the project meant that some people were excluded from the excavation it also proved to be a positive boon to others. John Lorimer, the circle's discoverer, was just looking for an excuse to follow the whole process through and an offer to be a 'runner' for the cameraman was just what was needed. 'I jumped at the opportunity', writes John, 'as I would have a good reason to be on site. I telephoned the cameraman, Graham Johnston, who asked if they could film me – they were pleased to have me on board as the finder and as a local. As a result I carried equipment for both Graham and his soundman, Alan. I was very excited to see the process from start to finish', continues John, 'seeing the first posts taken out, and later, at Flag Fen, seeing it being cleaned for the first time, revealing the axe marks as if they had been made yesterday'.

However, Mick Aston, along with the other team members, took the exclusion from the dig in his stride and instead busied himself researching

the other aspects of the monument. The timbers that had already been lifted from the site had been transferred to the laboratories at Flag Fen and it was here that the members of 'Time Team' went to discover what, if anything, the archaeologists had managed to find out that would aid the building of a reconstruction. At Flag Fen the team members met up with Maisy Taylor, an archaeological director of the site and acknowledged expert in ancient timbers, who led them through the findings so far. As it transpired the timbers yielded far more information than was first thought possible.

In the site laboratories Maisy Taylor was able to point out to members of the team the original working marks that were still clearly visible on the sections of excavated timber. These markings, left by the builders' bronze tools, are believed to be the earliest such markings discovered in England. Furthermore, by cross referencing the surviving tool markings with excavated examples it was possible to say that the tool used to shape the timbers was an axe; an axe that was similar, but by no means identical, to that discovered by John Lorimer on Holme beach the previous spring. Maisy was also keen to establish any possible hazards that the timbers may have presented. 'She asked me if there was anything likely to come out of the wood', writes John Lorimer, 'that could give a bite or a sting – I said no. "Anything with tentacles?" she asked. No, I replied. "So what is that coming out of the timber?" says she – I looked at it, grabbed and pulled out a King Rag Worm – a kind of water dwelling millipede, which can grow to about one inch long with a half inch girth – which would have had a nasty nip had it been alive'.

Maisy Taylor was also able to shed much light on the actual timbers themselves, identifying them as oak and explaining that, from the remains of thefinal growth ring, it was possible to deduce that they had been felled in the spring. She had also managed to identify a fibrous material, discovered wound through a hole in the central oak, as thick strands of honeysuckle.

These strands, discovered buried deep alongside the half buried timber, had come to light during the trial excavation the previous winter. Those now involved with the excavation, she pointed out, believed that the honeysuckle had been used as some form of rope and was probably left in place after dragging the main stump into position. Armed with this new information the members of *Time Team* departed to begin their attempt at reconstructing the circle.

Apple Henge

he first task that faced the experts from *Time Team* was recreating the actual tools needed to do the job. It was impractical to fell all the timber needed for the reconstruction using replica tools but, in the spirit of experimental archaeology, it was felt that it should be attempted on the central oak at the very least. The team first needed to have replicas cast of the Bronze Age axe, as identified by Maisy Taylor, that had been used by the original builders of the circle. This was done using a method that closely resembled the ways that Bronze Age man would have had available to him and the result was several very wicked looking axe heads. Once these had been cleaned up, sharpened, and mounted on their handles the team were ready to begin.

To reconstruct the timber circle *Time Team* first needed to fell the trees that were to be used for the main timbers. For an accurate portrayal of the monument the team needed to cut down one 150 year old oak and twenty smaller trees. These trees came from managed woodland in Bromley, south east London, and under the guidance of Damien Goodburn, the team's woodworking expert, the felling took place using a mixture of ancient and modern techniques. The main oak, to be later used as the central stump, was felled by hand with the replica Bronze Age axes playing a leading role. In fact, several members of the team expressed surprise at just how effective the replica axes actually were. They were by no means as useful as the modern steel axes but, compared to the flint axe knapped by Phil

Harding, they showed themselves to be a vast improvement.

Phil Harding, a field archaeologist from Wessex Archaeology and long term member of the *Time Team*, has spent many years studying ancient flint tools and in the process of his research he has become one of England's most respected flint knappers. With a keen interest in experimental archaeology, Phil had recreated a flint axe, the fore runner of the bronze axes used to build Seahenge, and had put it to use during the felling of the large oak. Although a relatively successful experiment, the axe performing well in the circumstances, the flint axe was nowhere near as practical as the replicas of the later bronze axes. It is through experiments such as those carried out by Phil Harding that we can achieve a much greater understanding of exactly how important the introduction of metal tools was to our ancestors.

Once the trees for the reconstruction had been felled the members of the *Time Team* had one more experiment to carry out before they began work on the reconstruction proper. They had decided to test the archaeologists theories concerning the thick strands of honeysuckle discovered by the central stump and intended to make their own 'rope' of honeysuckle with which to drag the newly felled oak. Calling in further expert help the team managed to produce a fair facsimile of the honeysuckle 'rope' found at Holme but were much less successful in using it to drag the tree stump. After only a few tugs the honeysuckle gave way. However, the team theorised that the honeysuckle they were using was too dry to be of any use. Had it been wet, or even soaked in water, it may very well have produced a much stronger rope. When later put to the test this theory proved correct and a wet honeysuckle rope was discovered to be most effective.

With the work at Bromley completed, the felled timbers were transported back to Norfolk where the team were to begin building their reconstruction. The site chosen for this new monument was in the corner of an apple orchard at Thornham, a few miles to the east of Holme-Next-The-Sea, owned by local landowner Andrew Jamieson. Working over a single weekend *Time Team* first marked out the shape of the monument on the ground before digging a trench in which the outer palisade of timbers

would be placed. John Lorimer was on site throughout the entire process and got involved with much of the work firsthand. 'Hardwood wedges were used to split the logs for finger posts', he writes, '(and) I cleaned the soil and stones out of the roots to make it lighter. Damien used a replica axe, similar to the kind that had been used to build the original circle, to trim the stump and posts and to cut the eyelet which was needed for towing the main stump into place and also used an adze to dress the timbers'.

The timbers for the outer palisade had to be, quite literally, manhandled into position. 'With the timbers all lying down, split and ready to be positioned in the trench, we had not realised – until we picked up the first one – how high the circle would be or indeed how difficult it would be to manoeuvre the heavy timbers into position – with much pushing and shoving we finally got them into place'.

Then, as the first of the split logs for the outer circle were manoeuvred into position, the hole for the central stump was excavated. 'Lard greased logs were used as skids for the stump', continues John Lorimer, 'which weighed about one and a half tons, to slide it into position. We had to tow it about forty feet using a ten foot long honeysuckle rope, long enough for six men – three on either side – to get a good hold of, to drop it into its hole'. Using more, and better constructed, honeysuckle ropes the team members, helped by many others, managed to drag the central stump into the circle where it was gently manoeuvred into the hole. 'There were two men either side and two at the rear armed with poles to keep it on course', says John, 'this was achieved far more easily than had been anticipated'. Once in place it was discovered that the rope, attached through a hole cut in the stump, was going to prove very difficult to remove. The team members decided instead to leave it in place; just as the original builders of Seahenge had done over four thousand years before.

The reconstruction in the orchard at Thornham, or 'Apple Henge' as many locals now refer to it, took only a single weekend to complete yet the repercussions continued for many months afterwards. A considerable number of those who actually watched the 'Christmas special' when it was first broadcast on December 29th were not happy with the way it had portrayed the events surrounding the excavation at Holme or the way in which the reconstruction had been produced. The cameraman, Graham Johnson, had followed much of the debate as it unfolded and had even been with the protesters when they began their attempted legal action, but it was felt by many that the view given by the programme was biased and one sided.

To the protesters, both those from Holme itself and those from further afield, the *Time Team* programme was believed to have been the subject of extreme editorial bias. Stephanie Middleton, a local woman with strong views upon the circle's removal, writes that the programme left her 'Very disappointed. Again an advert for English Heritage. Local interviews were obviously edited out. Surely we as locals should have had our say'. Geoff Needham, Chairman of the Holme Parish Council, also described himself as 'disappointed' by the editing of the show. 'Knowing how much footage Graham Johnson took', writes Geoff, 'I felt the editor took a light hearted look at the story that unfolded on our beach, and did not really do it justice'.

Even John Lorimer, the discoverer of the circle on the beach, was not entirely happy with the finished result. 'Johnny Spencer, a conceptual artist friend', writes John Lorimer, 'commented that the programme "was a bit disappointing because they had made it into a fun thing for all the family". Having experienced some harassment as a result of the subsequent controversy and media circus following my discovery I was reluctant to have my name used by *Time Team* who were therefore unable to show some footage that might have revealed a fuller explanation of the find and interpretation of the site itself. This may have contributed', continues John, 'to the programme seeming rather low brow'. However, John believes that many useful things did come out of the filming and was happy to have been involved. He writes that 'the filming was useful in demonstrating the problems that can beset such an excavation and the constructing of the replica at Thornham by numerous experts in different fields using contemporary tools gave a valuable insight into Bronze Age technology'.

The Trouble With Trees

Although the protesters at Holme were unhappy at the way the debate had been portrayed on the programme there were many more who were outraged at the felling of the trees used for the reconstruction. The idea that yet more mature trees had to be felled simply to satisfy the viewers of a television programme went against many of the beliefs that the Seahenge protesters held dear. Many of them, in particular the Druids and spiritualists, saw the emergence of the oak circle at Holme as a symbol of their ongoing battle to save the dying oaks of Britain; to discover that yet more trees had been felled simply to reconstruct something that they truly believed should never have been removed in the first place left them feeling outraged.

Sam Jones, the co-ordinator of the 'Friends of Seahenge' campaign, was particularly upset by the damage she believed the programme caused. She later described watching the programme as 'awful – I cried all over again. I felt they were insensitive – their care for nature was appalling. It was heartbreaking', she continues, 'to see those beautiful trees being cut down'. Sam, however, was not the only person to be upset by the felling of the trees. The London borough of Bromley, in whose jurisdiction the trees originally stood, were also less than impressed with the actions of *Time Team*. The trees, they insisted, were 'in a wood within Bromley Borough where all trees are protected by tree preservation orders'. 'Time Team' had, in effect, cut down the trees without permission and in direct conflict with the borough's preservation orders.

As this news came to light, barely three weeks after the screening of the programme on television, it began to look as though the popular archaeologists had finally gone too far. Robin Cooper, the head of heritage for Bromley council, was reported as saying that 'no consent was given for the felling to take place and the council will now be considering whether to prosecute those involved in authorising and undertaking the work'. With the programme already stirring up yet more debate about the circle's removal the very last thing that the Channel Four producers of the series needed was a high profile legal case. However, as things turned out the members of the team may not have been operating quite as far outside the law as some people would have us believe.

It later transpired that the woodland site in Bromley from which the timbers were taken was managed for conservation purposes and that the landowner, whose family have managed the same site for several centuries, did have a licence to carry out timber clearance. The management, renewal and coppicing of the woodland has been highly successful in the past, demonstrated by the return of several native animal and plant species, and all activity on the site is designed to be environmentally stable. Unfortunately, the owner's licence had expired a few short weeks before the programme was made.

Damien Goodburn, the teams expert on woodworking techniques, was keen to point out that the work they carried out in the Kentish woodland was done with only the best intentions in mind. Writing on the *Time Team* web page devoted to Seahenge and its surrounding debate Damien is reported as saying that '*Time Team* would never use materials that were not obtained in a sustainable manner'. When questioned about the actual trees themselves he writes that 'the twenty young oaks came from an area of coppiced woodland; all of them will regrow from the stumps. The mature oak stood in a particularly dark area of woodland in which selective felling was needed to let in light to the forest floor and encourage the growth of smaller fauna and less mature trees. Particular care was taken', he continues, 'during the felling of the large oak to protect a mature rowan tree growing in its shadow. Like the oak, the rowan is considered by some to have magical, or spiritual, significance. It will now flourish where once the oak stood'.

Bromley council representatives have since met with all those involved in the felling of thetrees and the whole incident has been thoroughly investigated. It appears unlikely, considering the nature of the managed woodland, that any further action will be taken against the programme makers. The incident has, they believe, been blown out of all proportion

and insiders at Channel Four are reported as saying that they believe 'someone's trying to stir it up'. However, putting aside the legalities the question remains; was the building of the *Time Team* replica circle worth the sacrifice of the trees that were felled to build it? Did those involved really learn anything that they did not know before, or could not have learnt from the felling of a single tree? Opinion is divided.

John Lorimer, who witnessed most of the events involved, feels that the building of the replica was entirely worthwhile. 'Watching the circle being replicated', he writes, 'feeling its size and dimensions, and standing in the centre with the bole in place, was exhilarating – the joint effort gave everyone a huge sense of achievement and awe at what they had originally created. Damien passed around a bottle of homebrew liqueur and we toasted with champagne and cake. Tony Robinson approached me and asked how I felt about it all, to which I could only reply – gobsmacked'.

What
Was
Seahenge?

CHAPTER 8

When all the arguments and debates have been put aside and forgotten the one question that remains is the circle itself. We know when it was built, the tools that were used and even how it was put together, but what was it actually for? What was Seahenge?

Since the very first appearance of the circle in the early summer of 1998 many different ideas have been put forward concerning the actual use that the circle was put to and what part it played in the life of early Bronze Age man. Some of the ideas and suggestions have been plausible and attractive; others outlandish and some just plain silly. All of the suggestions, no matter how weird and wonderful, have, at one time or another, received coverage in the media and have further added fuel to the debate surrounding the monument. Some of the suggestions have been put forward by archaeologists, others by interested outside observers and a few have even been proposed

through the letters pages of the local newspapers. It is perhaps worth recording the suggestions that have received the most public acclaim in some detail.

To begin with there is the most obvious suggestion, and one that will probably continue to surface from time to time due to the monuments early christening by the media as Seahenge. The idea that the circle is some sort of 'henge' monument is still strong in the public's mind and as long as the name endures so will the idea. Unfortunately, the circle, though bearing some obvious physical similarities to sites such as Stonehenge, does not contain the most basic requirements that define a 'henge'.

It is interesting to note that the actual name 'henge', although today given a fairly strict archaeological definition, was originally derived from Stonehenge itself. The massive and brooding stone circle on Salisbury plain was as much of a mystery to the early British chroniclers as it is today but, even by the time of the Norman conquest, the site was known as 'Stanhengues'. Wace, the Anglo-Norman chronicler, writing in the twelfth century, claimed that the monument was known as 'the hanging stones' (the literal Anglo-Norman translation of 'Stan-hengues') in both England and Normandy. A few decades later Henry of Huntingdon records that the name was well deserved as the stones 'hang as it were in the air'.

Others have preferred to think that the term 'hanging stones', rather than referring to their marvellous construction, actually harks back to a time when criminals were executed at the site. Geoffrey of Monmouth, the great mediaeval historian, went further still; claiming that the site was named after the Saxon warlord Hengist who had slaughtered dozens of British warriors on the spot. The circle was re-erected, having been brought from Ireland, with the aid of Merlin the magician, as their lasting memorial. Whatever the true original source of the name it was eventually corrupted over time and 'Stanhengues' became the more English 'Stone-henge'.

As time passed ever onwards the people who saw the mon-ument once more tried to fathom the true meaning of its name. The stones in the title were obvious to even the most unlearned visitor and therefore the 'henge' part of the name, it was believed, must refer to the type of monument. It must mean, they deduced, that it was a 'henge' made of stone. As the centuries have passed what started as 'fancy' has become fact and all such monuments are now referred to as 'Henges'. However, as the years passed so the definition of a 'henge' became more specific and the circle at Holme no longer falls into this category.

A 'henge' is today defined as a large circular earth bank with a ditch on the inside. These monuments are believed to have been ceremonial in nature, rather than of any defensive usage, and the central area was often left clear for communal activities. Most 'henge' monuments are found in low lying areas close to water sources and it is believed that they were employed in some form of open air cult associated with water. Upon occasion round barrows, or burial mounds, have been discovered within the circles; perhaps linking the world of the living with the dead. Some henges do have circles of either timber or stone around them but this is not necessarily the case. Henges are also often discovered in small groups, rather than alone, such as the three discovered at Thornborough in Yorkshire and the four found at

Priddy on the Mendip Hills of Somerset. The henge monuments of England also pre-date the circle at Holme by many centuries.

Henge type structures are not limited solely to England or even the British Isles. Similar sites have been discovered throughout Europe and, more surprisingly, as far afield as North America. The following extract, though it could easily be referring to a British henge, was actually written about a monument erected by the Adena Indians in Ohio in about 400 BC :-

The earthwork enclosures appear to be ceremonial constructions rather than defence works. Many are almost perfectly circular. These 'sacred circles' average 100 metres in diameter and are enclosed by low embankments with the 'moats' for these embankments within rather than outside the circle. Gateways open through the embankments. Burial mounds sometimes have been found inside the circles, and there are instances where several such circles were constructed together at a single site.

(G.R. WILEY – An introduction to American Archaeology, 1966)

If the circle discovered at Holme is not a 'henge' then what is it? John Lorimer, the discoverer of the monument, along with many others who saw the original photograph, believed that it could well have been the remains of a Bronze Age dwelling of some sort. This view was shared by many people locally, including Geoff Needham, and it remained popular for many weeks. Given the limited nature of the original information this was not an unreasonable initial conclusion. The small size of the circle, though impossible to gauge from the photograph alone, was more reminiscent of a late Neolithic or Bronze Age 'round house' than of the massive ceremonial structures at Avebury and Stonehenge. The remains of such dwellings have come to light before, though usually only as a series of post holes from which the timbers have decayed, and the circle at Holme was approximately the right size and shape. Further than this the outer circle could well have been the remains of a wall and the central trunk could have been the central 'crown' post that supported the roof structure.

Although this suggestion was discounted at a fairly early stage in the investigation, the circle's similarities to other known structures did prompt further suggestions along similar lines. One of the least romantic ideas, and one that led to a small debate within a debate, first came to light via the letters page of the Eastern Daily Press. A correspondent suggested that the monument at Holme bore an uncanny resemblance to structures that he had seen, and were still visible, in Ireland. These structures, often built of stone and with a central platform, were used as enclosures in which cattle were kept. The outer stockade kept the cattle contained and away from harm while the central platform was used to spread fodder upon. This rather unexciting view of the timber circle at Holme, though soon discarded by archaeologists, did capture the imagination of the more 'henge' weary readers of the paper and a short, and not entirely serious, exchange of letters was soon forthcoming.

By June the 21st 1999, the day of the midsummer solstice, the Eastern Daily Press had one more possible explanation of the timber circles actual purpose to offer its readers. Anthony Ward, a keen amateur sailor and expert in celestial navigation techniques, was featured in the paper putting forward his new theory concerning the role of the timber circle. Mr Ward, who lives in Norwich, believed that the circle was originally constructed as a solar calendar designed to mark the longest day of the year. He further suggested that the inverted oak at the circle's centre, rather than being an altar, was a marker point for the only place on the Norfolk landscape where the sun rises over the sea. Anyone standing by the circle on midsummer morning would actually be able to watch the sun rise over the sea; something that only happens, he claimed, for a few days each year.

Mr Ward believed that the few days a year, at the summer solstice, when the sun rises in the same spot over the sea would have been a significant date for the ancient builders of the site. From this point the Bronze Age people would have been able to accurately calculate their calendar. Mr Ward went on to point out that the siting of the circle was no accident. The discovery of this one spot on the coastline would not have been easy and the circle was constructed to accurately mark its position.

Although Anthony Ward's theories remain unproven they did attract a great deal of interest and much popular support amongst the Spiritualists and Druids who had gathered at the circle to celebrate the solstice. Sam Jones, the co-ordinator of the Friends of Seahenge campaign to block the circles excavation, believed that Mr Ward's theory, though unproven, added weight to the argument against the monuments removal. If the circle was removed then the theory could not be studied in the proper context of the surrounding landscape.

However, the popularity of Anthony Ward's theory was short lived. It had the advantage of having a mythic element to it but, as many people pointed out, the circle was now known to have been built at least a mile from the sea. It would have originally been too far away to obtain a clear view of the solstice sunrise, and furthermore, would have had its view obscured, if not entirely blocked, by sand dunes nearer the sea shore. As other, more literal minded, people pointed out; if you wish to watch the sun rise over the sea why not go to Great Yarmouth where they can see it every day. Mr Ward's theory, like those that had gone before, fell into disuse.

Death and Water

Finally, with theories and counter theories being put forward on almost a weekly basis, the archaeologists involved with the site's excavation made their views known to the world. David Miles, chief archaeologist at English Heritage, rather than putting forward a concise theory as to the circle's use, preferred to point out the possible significance of the various elements that made up the monument. He pointed out that the manner in which the palisade had been constructed, with the tree trunks split down the centre and the bark facing outwards, would have presented 'a barrier, with the outside looking like a continuous circle of bark'. 'You would have felt', he continued, 'as if you were standing in a hollowed out tree. From the outside, the circle would have looked like a huge tree trunk'.

David Miles then went on to point out that the central oak stump was of particular significance. 'The up-turned tree trunk', he stated, 'is interesting because that's something you get in mythology, from the Middle East to the Lap regions in northern Scandinavia'. The tree was seen as a route to the heavens and the underworld', he continued, 'so this was an evocative structure forming a symbolic tree which stood at the boundary of earth, sky and sea.

In Anglo-Saxon and Viking mythology there was something called the 'World Tree', an ash called 'Ygdrasil' which supported the world and the heavens, In Indo-European mythology there is the idea of the sacred oak. This monument is probably part of this complex mythical structure'.

When questioned about the actual use that the circle was put to David Miles also had his own

theory. The upside down tree trunk could, he believed, have been used as an altar, or platform, on which the bodies of the dead were laid. This would allow the body to decay in the open air and, with the aid of scavenging birds, the bones would have soon been picked clean. This method of removing the corrupt flesh from the bones, which were often then preserved separately or even cremated, is thought to have helped to speed the soul of the departed to the afterlife.

This method of dealing with the physical remains of the dead by exposing their bodies to the elements, or 'excarnation' as it is more properly known, is believed to have been carried out at various periods in history throughout Britain and Europe. It appears to have been based upon the belief that the flesh, which deteriorates rapidly after death, is essentially corrupt. By removing the flesh, or allowing it to be removed, the spirit of the dead person would be liberated from the confines of the body. Although little is known about the belief system that accompanied the practice, various theories having been put forward, it is an idea that has re-appeared in various cultures all over the globe. Until very recent times the practice was still carried out by some of the woodland tribes of North American Indians and several distinct and separate island cultures.

The theory that found favour with David Miles was also popular with many of the other archaeologists involved with the timber circle at Holme. Dr Francis Pryor, a Director of Archaeology at Flag Fen and an authority on the Bronze Age, also believed that the circle was closely connected with death and funerary rites. 'We are not absolutely sure', he is reported as saying, 'what these people thought that next world was, but we think they envisaged a parallel world inhabited by their ancestors'. Dr Pryor was particularly interested in the inverted oak at the circles centre. 'We often find', he stated, 'everyday objects deliberately turned upside down at Bronze Age sites. The inverted oak is a very complex statement. It is the world turned upside down, just as death is an inversion of life'.

Controversially, Dr Pryor also believed that the site of the circle, and its position in relation to the surrounding landscape, was just as important and significant as the circle itself. He stated that he believed that Bronze Age man would have been aware of the obvious symbolism of the coastline as a divider between the two worlds, land and sea, life and death, and the circle, situated at the boundary, would have marked both the place and the state of transition. This view, though not shared by many other archaeologists, may go some way to explaining and understanding the mind of Bronze Age people, and in particular their view of death and the afterlife.

The theory that the site was used for the purposes of 'excarnation' is one that has found popularity with both the archaeologists and public alike and, at the time of writing, it is the generally accepted theory as to the circles use. Such sites have even been discovered before and, as Mark Brennand from theNorfolk Archaeological Unit is reported as saying, 'the sites of timber circles are not uncommon, but up until now all we have seen are the soil markings where the timbers once stood before they crumbled away. Here,' he continued, 'the circle was built on waterlogged ground so it's never dried out and the timbers have been preserved'. The very fact that several other similar monuments have been discovered; some of which appear to have been far more elaborate than the circle at Holme, indicates that the practice of excarnation may have been a widespread funerary rite throughout late Neolithic and Early Bronze Age Britain.

One of the most elaborate, and best documented, sites that is associated with excarnation is to be found in Wiltshire near to both Avebury and Stonehenge. Known as the 'Sanctuary' the site was rediscovered and excavated in 1930 by eminent archaeologist Maud Cunnington. Lying alongside the Ridgeway, an ancient trackway, the Sanctuary appears to have been first constructed in about 2900 BC, nearly a millennia before Seahenge, and was approximately ten metres

in diameter. The outer wall consisted of twelve large oak posts that were set into the ground and surrounded an inner ring of eight somewhat smaller posts. This inner ring, it is believed, may have supported a partial thatched roof that stretched around the outer edge of the structure; leaving a large central area open to the elements. The monument was rebuilt several times during its lifetime, the last time being in about 2300 BC, and each time the structure was slightly enlarged or improved upon.

Although similar to several other known late Neolithic round houses it is unlikely that the Sanctuary was a dwelling of any sort. The lack of domestic waste, evidence of hearth fires and rubbish pits points to it having been of a ritualistic nature. This idea is also supported by the large number of burials discovered in the immediate vicinity; an indication the site was associated with death. It is believed that the site was constructed as some form of mortuary house in which the bodies of the dead could be stored until the rotting flesh had been cleansed from the bones. The large central opening in the roof could well have been to allow the elements and scavenging birds to attack the corpse while the stockade walls kept the larger predators at bay.

The actual process of 'excarnation' is not a particularly simple one and it is unlikely that it was carried out in the case of every corpse. It is quite possible that the practice of 'excarnation' was only used on the more important members of the tribe; leaving the mere commoners bodies to be either burned or buried. By looking at certain other world cultures that still carried out this practice until relatively recent times it is possible to get an understanding of what was actually involved in the process.

On the island of Malekula in the New Hebrides the native population continued to use 'excarnation' upon the bodies of their departed until well into the nineteenth century. The rituals associated with it were long and complex and, as such, they were only performed upon the bodies of the tribal elders and chiefs. The corpse, attended by the local priests, would be laid out on a raised scaffold, much as done by several North American Indian tribes, and there it would be watched over while it decayed. The process would be hastened by the continual washing of the body; again linking the idea of water and death, and the villagers would take part in ritual washing of their own bodies to cleanse themselves from the 'sickness of death'. Eventually, encouraged by the continual immersion in water the body would decompose and the villagers then held a feast to celebrate the lower jaw dropping from the skull; with which the soul of the dead person departed to the afterlife.

From evidence discovered at other sites in Britain it appears likely that the bones of the departed, once cleaned of the corrupting flesh, were then subjected to further ritual. Several sites have produced evidence that indicate that the cleansed bones were then subjected to prolonged heating. The bones, rather than being burnt, as would be the case in cremation, simply show scorch marks and slight charring. At Temple Bottom near Avebury, West Kennet long barrow, Tinkinswood, Randwick and Stoney Littleton, burials have been discovered that all show signs of having been scorched after the flesh was removed. No evidence has been found that indicates that there was any burning at the burial site itself and it must therefore be assumed that the bones were only interred after the heating had been carried out at another site. It may well be that this practice was carried out to thoroughly dry the bones, evaporating the moisture in the bone marrow, and so help to ensure their preservation.

Spirit Goods?

John Lorimer, the original finder of the bronze axe that led to the circle's discovery, now also favours the idea that the circle was used for 'excarnation'. Having been involved with the project since the very beginning he has been witness to all the events as they unfolded and has heard just about all the theories that have been put forward. Having kept in close contact with the archaeologists John has seen more of the evidence than most and now firmly believes that the circle 'was probably used for sacred funereal rites'. However, John Lorimer's story, and the story of the circle he discovered, does not end with the removal of the timbers from the beach at Holme.

John Lorimer remained a frequent visitor to the site while the excavation was in progress and, at the suggestion of Gary Hibbard, the site warden, even became a part time warden to help protect the reserve from the increased number of visitors. 'Whilst performing this pleasant task', writes John, 'I was able to observe the site and discovered and collected some unusual smashed stones under the sand, close by the site'. The discovery of these 'stones' so near to the circle encouraged John to keep his eyes open for any other unusual items and the stones became a fairly frequent find. 'They came', John continues, 'from a common source on the seaward side of the circle. . . Some were clearly charred; some were possibly man made, some of the rock had clearly been 'knapped' and ground down by human hands – many had a curious 45 degree angle'.

The stones were not the only items that John discovered and he was soon making regular finds of pottery as well. These fragments of broken pot also came from a site very close to the circle and John made an effort to collect as many pieces as he could in between the tides. However John was not interested in collecting the pottery sherds simply as souvenirs. 'When Mark Brennand and a colleague visited', writes John, 'I informed him of my finds, gave him a large box of these stones and pottery and showed him where to look. His colleague came over and asked what we were doing, bent down and found a piece of middle to late Bronze Age 'pinched' pottery. They found another piece when they did a small excavation'. Since the removal of the circle timbers John Lorimer has continued to discover pottery fragments at the site. Although some of the sherds actually fit together the evidence indicates that there was more than one pot and that they come from quite a wide time span. The pots appear to have been fairly typical 'coiled' Bronze Age pots, built up by hand rather than on a wheel. Other visitors to the site have also discovered pottery fragments, many of which have been handed to the archaeologists, and it is hoped that they will be able to produce drawings of the original vessels from the evidence given by the surviving fragments.

The pottery fragments and unusually shaped stones have continued to be found by John at Holme beach and these have recently been accompanied by other, more mysterious, finds. Lying near where he found the pottery fragments John has discovered small pieces of charcoal, large fragments of bone and pieces of wood bark. These, along with all the other items found on the beach, were duly handed in to the archaeologists.

The archaeologists then informed John that the pots may well have been 'cremation urns'; vessels in which the cremated remains of individual bodies were placed before final burial. It appears to have been a common practice at the time to place the remaining fragments of bone in an urn, cover the opening with bark, and then bury them upside down. These funerary urns are also most usually discovered in a broken state and it has been suggested that the urns were actually broken intentionally after they were placed in the ground. It could well be that the charcoal, bark and pottery fragments discovered by John are the remains of just such a practice.

However, the bone that John discovered on the beach has since been identified as being from a sheep and no human remains have, as yet, been discovered. However, John continued to discover other pieces of bone which have also been identified as belonging to animals rather than humans. Among the numerous fragments have been found the remains of badgers, roe deer, partridges, cattle and pigs. This fact, combined with the evidence that is now coming to light at the site, suggests a slightly different interpretation. Almost every item discovered by John Lorimer and the archaeologists on the beach has been damaged or defaced in some way. Even the curious stones with the 45 degree angle have been either smashed or damaged and only one has

been discovered whole. The axe head that John found was also damaged; a chip having been hammered into the cutting edge, and it now appears likely that all the damage was caused intentionally by the original builders and users of the circle.

Such practices, of destroying items before burial, have been recorded at many other sites from the period and it appears to have been carried out in a ritual manner. It is now thought that this practice is closely linked with the funerary rites carried out at the time. The people appear to have believed that by destroying or defacing the items that they were burying they were releasing the spirit of the object; much as the removal of flesh from the bones released the spirit of the deceased. The spirit of these objects

Jackie Lorimer walks along the course of a 4000 year old timber causeway on Holme Beach copyright - J. Lorimer.

could then pass over into the afterlife for the use of the spirit of the departed. The items found by John could well be just such 'spirit goods', sacrificed to be passed over to the dead.

The pot fragments, the charcoal, the animal bones and the axe may well have been gifts to the departed soul; allowing them to make fire, carry water, cook their meals and cut firewood. The curiously shaped stones may well have been 'pot boilers'; hard stones that were heated in the fire before being dropped into a vessel to warm its contents, the pottery of the period having little resistance to direct heat due to its unfired nature. The fact that some of these 'pot boilers' appear to have been 'made' of clay, making their use impractical, further supports the idea of their use being purely ceremonial.

However, the presence of such spirit items need not necessarily indicate that there are human remains nearby. When excavating the sites of Bronze Age round barrows, most notably at Willy Howe, Gib Hill and Wold Newton in the north of England, archaeologists discovered just such collections of 'Spirit goods', including animal bones, hazel wood, charcoal and burnt flints, but in none of these sites was there any sign of a body. Furthermore, there was no evidence that any of these sites had ever contained a body or the remains of a human cremation. They were simply burial sites for the spirit items, not the deceased.

The idea that the items discovered by John Lorimer and the archaeologists at the site could indeed be spirit goods is an interesting one. The items were discovered near to, but not within, the area once occupied by the circle and indicates that the importance of the site may well extend beyond the area immediately surrounding the lifted monument. The fact that such a large number of individual finds have been made in the same area also belies the argument that they are single objects washed out of the circle by the tide. The new finds are appearing from under the peat and sand; indicating that they are actually in their original positions. Taken together the new finds tend to lead one to the conclusion that the site goes far beyond the circle, both in terms of area and significance, and that the timber circle is only one small part of a much larger whole; a supposition that has recently been proved correct.

Back in the late 1970s Geoff Needham, a resident of Holme, was walking along the beach about half a mile from where the Seahenge timbers were later to emerge. Geoff knew the area very well indeed, having spent many hours walking the foreshore, and was interested to note a series of timbers that appeared to be emerging from the beach. The timbers were in a rough circle and appeared to Geoff as being very old indeed. Being interested in the local history of the area, and not recognising the feature, Geoff contacted the county archaeologists. However, after a cursory inspection the archaeologist who visited the site deemed the circle to be of little interest. Although some people claim that this was another appearance of John Lorimer's circle it is now widely believed that Geoff Needham discovered a second 'Seahenge'; a feature that the archaeologists of the time failed to recognise.

Strange Landscape

The actions of the sea and sand upon the peat layers at Holme Dunes are most curious. As the tides roll in over the area of exposed peat the waters carry with them thousands of particles of sand. It is this sand, suspended in the water as it rolls back and forth, that is actually responsible for bringing many of the new objects to light. As it washes back and forth over the delicate peat it acts very much like sand paper; scouring away a thin layer of peat particles each time. Storm tides and heavy weather only add to this effect, breaking off larger chunks of peat and washing it out to sea. Gradually, over a period of months, or even years, the landscape that has been built up by time is gradually being stripped back layer by layer. As each new area of peat is eroded a strange new landscape is emerging; a landscape from our distant past.

It is within this peat layer that the original surface landscape that formed the very ground upon which Seahenge's builders stood is located. Gradually, the salt-marsh that they walked upon is coming to the surface and it is bringing with it some amazing discoveries. It is this marsh surface that first brought to light John Lorimer's axe head, then Seahenge itself, then the pottery sherds, animal bones and charcoal.

Now, as another autumn and winter has passed, the peat is beginning to reveal even more artefacts and, of profound significance, other timber structures. Seahenge was not alone; was not a single great find in an eroded landscape but rather the first great artefact from an emerging ancient landscape.

John Lorimer, in his many visits to the site, has actually watched the process happen. It is a sight that few men will ever really witness; nature itself revealing the past, piece by piece and layer by layer. As John has patiently observed as the months have passed the sea and sand have become the archaeologists, gradually bringing to light a four thousand year old landscape. The landscape of Seahenge's builders.

One of the first major features to be noticed by John, and subsequently by the archaeologists, was that there were areas in the surface where no peat was actually present. Instead there were long thin areas covered with small rounded stones. These stones, rather than being part of the original marsh, are actually the beds of ancient streams and small rivers that ran through the salt-marsh on their way to the sea. The first of these ancient and shallow river beds that came to light actually ran between the site of the circle and the peat scarps; the peat scarps that had been producing animal bones and other 'spirit goods'.

Then, in the area of the peat scarp itself, on the other side of the old river bed from the circle, a second timber structure began to emerge. Although much smaller than the original circle this new structure was also obviously man made. The structure was also much simper than the circle. All it consisted of was two lengths of timber, logs that had been worked by axes, that were laid on their side next to each other. The upper surfaces had been squared off and the whole was surrounded by what appeared to be a small wickerwork fence.

The presence of the wicker work surrounding the object immediately aroused suspicions that it may have been some sort of fish trap. However, further analysis revealed that the wickerwork fence was actually constructed of oak withies. Wicker-work and basket-work can be done using a variety of types of timber. Willow, hazel and even honeysuckle will all work well and stand up to the rigours of time; oak, however, will not and will quickly become brittle as it naturally dries out in the atmosphere. The use of oak in the wicker fence clearly points to it being used not for any practical purpose but rather for its ritual significance.

The use of specific timbers, and most especially oak, in sites of ritual and ceremonial importance is well recorded among many ancient peoples. The Celtic peoples worship of the oak tree is well attested both in Britain and on the continent and their word for a sanctuary (Nemeton) appears to be identical in origin to the Latin Nemus, or wooded grove. The German tribes were particularly strong in their worship of trees and had harsh laws that protected them. Any man discovered to have removed the bark

from a living tree was to have his navel cut out and nailed to the area from which he had stripped the bark. The unfortunate culprit was then forced to go round and round the tree until his entrails were wound around the trunk; the mans skin and guts replacing the lost bark, a life for a life.

The Scandinavians also held trees in particular reverence. The Finnish tribes were known to have carried out their acts of worship in sacred groves until relatively recent centuries. Their sacred sites were almost always surrounded by a fence, past which no woman could go, and consisted of a clearing surrounded by a few sacred trees. It is also recorded that these trees were used to hang up the skins of

Another timber monument appears from the sand and peat. The two logs are both embedded in the clay and have been flattened along their top surfaces copyright - J. Lorimer.

their sacrificial victims and that no tree within the grove should be harmed in any way. Also in Scandinavia, at Upsala in Sweden, there was a very well known, and reputedly powerful, sacred grove in which every tree was regarded as divine.

Alongside the discovery of the two tree trunks within the wicker-work oak fence other timber artefacts and structures began to emerge from the peat beds at Holme. Across the surface of what would have been salt-marsh 4000 years ago the archaeologists found what appeared to be other timbers. These timbers, far from being just scattered remains, were laid out in a series of long lines and, in conjunction with wooden planks, some of which have also been discovered, may well have been pathways, or causeways, across the marsh.

The causeways, though just as likely to have been of a purely practical nature, may well have been ceremonial walkways between the timber structures. Some appear to point in the direction of known structures while others veer off across the marsh; heading no one knows where. It is possible that they connect the Seahenge site with other similar sites, such as the circle discovered by Geoff Needham in the late 1970s about half a mile along the beach. Perhaps there are more such structures still waiting to come to light, or perhaps, like Geoff Needham's circle, they have already been lost to the sea.

John Lorimer, amongst others, believes he does know what these other finds signify and in what way they join to form a whole. 'I imagine', writes John, 'the cadaver was first positioned upon the two logs and rites were held before they were ferried across the river to the circle. Once at the circle, having crossed the marsh on the causeways and waded through the river, the body was then placed on the central tree stump. After it had decomposed the bones were then removed and either buried or cremated. During the ceremony the spirit goods would be ritually broken and buried, their spirits going on to join the deceased in the afterlife'.

Although only speculation John Lorimer's ideas are based upon sound evidence and are tentatively shared by both historians and archaeologists. It is quite possible to conclude that what is appearing out of the peat at Holme is something more than just a simple circle constructed of ancient timbers. It may well be that Seahenge, Geoff Needham's circle, the wicker-work enclosure, the causeways, the riverbeds and the spirit goods all form part of one massive spiritual

The wickerwork enclosure surrounding the two logs. Unusually the uprights have been identified as 'alder' and the withies as 'oak'; a reversal of normal modern practice
copyright - J.Lorimer.

monument. Like Stonehenge, Avebury and the stone avenues that cover the Wiltshire countryside the area around Holme may have been just as large and just as important. Perhaps it was the religious site for the Bronze Age peoples of East Anglia; a place where they carried their important dead. A ritualistic landscape where the sea met the land and the bodies were ferried across to the sacred island in the marsh; an isle of the dead.

This is, of course, nothing but speculation. It is quite possible that future finds and further evidence will point to an entirely different conclusion. It may well be that the site proves to be nothing more than a place of funerary ritual, with no more spiritual significance that a modern hospital crematorium. However, at this moment in time it appears to be emerging as something more than just a place of crude biological death. Perhaps the site, against all my initial scepticism, really is a spiritual centre. Perhaps the Peddars Way, the ancient and mysterious track-way that stretches across the Norfolk landscape, does indeed lead somewhere after all. It leads to Holme.

88

Author's Note

At the time of going to press all the major timber structures discovered on Holme beach have now been either washed away, covered by the sand or removed by the archaeologists. There is nothing for the casual visitor to see and tourists are advised to stay away from the area for fear of further damage being caused to both the birdlife and their habitat.

Picture Overleaf - Tentative reconstruction of how the landscape at Holme may have looked about 4000 years ago copyright - Barnwell's Timescape

Who Built Seahenge?

n purely biological terms the people who actually built the monument at Holme Dunes that has become known as Seahenge were not very different from you or me. Considering the number of migrations, invasions and settlements that this land has been subject to in the intervening four millennia they were perhaps less genetically diverse but, in most other respects, we are the same. They were not less intelligent than us, they share the same feelings and fears that we do and, above all, they travelled the same journey of birth, life, love and death that we too must endure. It is only in the details; the beliefs that they held, the daily chores of survival and their expectations, that we differ. In all other respects we are one and the same.

However, it is in these details; in their attitudes to life and death, food and comfort, property and wealth, that we can begin to understand just how far, or how little, we have progressed in the intervening four thousand years. In purely technological terms we are their undoubted superiors, we have developed beyond their wildest imaginings, but how would they view our political, social and spiritual advances.

Have our attitudes to life and the world we live in really kept pace with our material progress. Have we become 'better' than them or, more simply, different?

It is first important to remember exactly how long ago the monument at Holme Dunes was actually built. The people that originally took their bronze axes to the oak trees that make up the circle in the spring of 2050 BC belong to the period known as the Early Bronze Age. Despite the Victorians tendency to lump together all those peoples of this island who were here before Caesar they were not the same people that met the Roman invaders on the beaches at Deal. Far

92

from it; by the time of the Roman invasion Seahenge was already two millennia old. The builders of Seahenge were as much a part of the distant past to the Romans as the Romans are to us. The builders of Seahenge belong to an even more ancient group of peoples than the Celts encountered by the legions and it would be misleading to even ascribe the term 'proto-Celts' to such a people. When Celtic civilisation was first emerging in central Europe the builders of Seahenge were already well established, with a well defined artistic style, distinct burial customs and identifiable cultural traits.

Seahenge was built at a time of great transition by a people who were one of the driving forces behind the changes that were taking place. However, the greatest change that was sweeping Europe, the introduction of the use of metals for tools and decorations, was not the rapid and abrupt change that many school books led us to believe. The discovery of bronze, and its introduction as a workable material,

did not happen overnight. Our ancestors were not simply stone tools users one day and then wielders of bronze axes the next. The transition took time, many centuries in some areas, and for a long period both metal and stone implements are found to have been used side by side. It is also misleading to think of the Late Stone Age leading gracefully into the Early Bronze Age. Such arbitrary dating is confusing and neglects the true transition period; the transition period that is now known as the 'Copper Age'.

Copper occurs as a natural and native metal; being found in small nugget form across a fairly widespread area, and is very malleable, or easily shaped. In fact raw copper is so easy to use and polish that its

Introduction may well have been of nothing more than a decorative nature to begin with. However, the early copper workers soon discovered that this bright new material had the advantage of making good quality tools; tools that could be re-smelted and reused once broken – a distinct advantage over their stone counterparts. The other obvious advantage must have been in the actual production methods used to create these tools. Stone tools had to be each individually fashioned, by an undoubtedly skilled craftsman, and would have taken many man hours to produce a single workable piece. Copper tools, on the other hand, could be cast in moulds, in a fraction of the time, and patterns could be duplicated again and again.

Unfortunately, the casting of pure copper is not as simple as I have made it sound. As a pure metal it lacks certain properties that allow it to flow easily through a mould and is vastly improved by the inclusion of a small amount of other elements. At some point the early copper using peoples discovered that by adding tin to the smelting process (ideally about ten per cent) they produced a much more easily cast alloy. As an added bonus it was soon realised that this new alloy, crude bronze, was also tougher than pure copper and kept a much sharper edge for a much longer time.

The Beaker People

At one and the same time as these great advances were being made in the field of metallurgy Europe was in a state of great upheaval. The various peoples of the region were probably under pressure from outside its geographical borders and, as a result, were on the move. Great migrations were taking place with entire populations gradually shifting and, as a result, gradually mixing with, and influencing, the new peoples that they came into contact with. One of these peoples, and one of the most important in the story of this island, were the 'Beaker People'.

The Beaker people, so named because of the distinctive beaker shape of their pottery vessels, appear to have originated in the area of modern Spain. They seem to have been accomplished metal workers, using both copper and gold, yet still continued to use flint for the more everyday items such as arrowheads and knives. They valued personal decoration, as shown by their use of jet and bone for buttons, and appear to have worn ear rings fashioned like little baskets of gold. Evidence points to them

having been experienced farmers, as well as herdsmen, and they favoured growing barley; it has even been suggested that they may well have discovered how to use the barley in the brewing of ale.

Why these people left the Iberian peninsular is a matter of some conjecture, but leave they did, first moving north and east into central Europe and then, at a later date, westwards to the shores of the Atlantic. From here it was a simple boat trip across the North Sea to Britain where they are already known to have been settled by 2500 BC in the southern and coastal regions. During their nomadic migration the Beaker people came into contact with many other peoples of Europe, influencing and in turn being influenced by, their varied and various cultures and it was the same when they reached these shores. The native population soon took to metal working, believed by some to have actually been introduced by the Beaker culture, and the newcomers soon adopted and adapted many of the local religious sites and customs.

Yet these early Beaker settlers were few in number and rather than an invasion of conquest the arrival of the Beaker people appears to have been a migration and assimilation. Evidence from burials does seem to indicate that these Beaker newcomers were physically slightly different from the native inhabitants of the region. They were taller, with a rounder head, and were much more thick set than the natives and in time, as their numbers increased, this undoubtedly gave them a physical edge. Combined with their metal working skills these large newcomers to Britain soon found themselves to be in command and evidence points to the likelihood that they became the overlords of the native population.

For about five centuries the Beaker culture appears to have been one of the dominant influences in southern and eastern Britain. They rebuilt Stonehenge, the great brooding monument on Salisbury Plain, adding the 'blue stones' from far away Wales and began the reconstruction of Avebury and Silbury Hill. Such great building programme indicate that they possessed an advanced agricultural system, with enough ready surplus of both food stuffs and time to invest many man hours in their monuments. They carried on animal husbandry, keeping both sheep and cattle for milk, cheese and hides as well as pigs for meat. They also used their spears and axes to hunt the native wildlife, in particular deer and wild boar. These tools also seem to have had their place in warfare and burial evidence indicates that their society was both male dominated and aggressive.

In terms of day to day living these Beaker peoples appear to have been little different from their predecessors. They seem to have still been semi-nomadic in nature; with few recorded permanent settlement sites, and to have constructed simple round houses in which to pass their winters. They were not prone to gathering in towns and cities, as their Mediterranean counterparts were beginning to do, and their largest settlements were probably no greater than a small village containing a few interrelated family units. It would only have been at times of festivals and rituals, such as at midsummer, when the whole tribe would have gathered together in celebration. In spiritual terms, however, they do appear to have been different from those that came before them. Evidence suggests that it was at this period that some form of sun worship, coupled with both water and death cults, began to supplant the ancient fertility cult of the mother goddess. Although not entirely abandoned; surviving in some forms down to the present day, the goddess seems to have greatly declined in importance.

The small details of everyday living, what they ate, what they drank and what they wore, are less easy to determine, let alone generalise about. We know that they kept herds of cattle and sheep and farmed them for milk, cheese, wool and leather as well as, upon occasion, meat. Evidence also indicates that they kept pigs; using them almost exclusively for meat production. As a by product the dried cattle manure was probably also a valuable source of fuel. Beyond this we can really say very little with any confidence. They did farm, that is without doubt, but beyond saying that they had some form of light plough and grew both barley and wheat, barley being by far the more popular crop, we cannot be sure.

That these early inhabitants of Britain harvested honey, probably from wild rather than domestic bees, is again a known fact; beakers having been discovered with the honey residue still intact, but whether they used it as a raw substance or rather to brew mead is open to conjecture. They already knew the rudiments of spinning and weaving, several fine woollen cloths having been discovered in graves, yet animal skins still appear to have been used for various articles of clothing. Leather belts have also been found; being fastened with carved toggles or crude buckles, and so it must be assumed that they were skilled in the arts of basic tanning. Decoration was probably important to them, as shown by the nature of their grave goods, and the discovery of long bronze pins in female burials has been suggested as indicating that the women wore their hair coiled up in a bun. Ear rings too are common finds, often being fashioned from pure gold, and we may suppose that they valued decoration as highly as we do today.

Their love of decoration can also be seen in the pottery that they produced. The most commonly discovered pots, the distinctive 'beakers' for which they are named, though varying slightly in design over the years, all show a great deal of decoration. This finely made pottery, far superior to its late Stone Age counterparts, was often covered with intricate geometric patterns that were incised and impressed into the surface. As well as forming the bulk of the everyday utensils these pots were of a high enough value to be commonly included amongst the burial goods taken with their owner into the afterlife.

As well as being farmers, warriors and herdsmen the Beaker people were also great traders. Evidence points to them having had complex and considerable trade links and importing artefacts from as far away as Ireland in the west, Scotland in the north and central Europe in the east. Their links with mainland Europe, forged at the time of their migration, seem to have been strong and trade between Britain and the mainland was continuous. Considering the fact that it was this people that brought the 'blue stones' for Stonehenge all the way from Wales it is unlikely that smaller trade goods would have presented them with any problems whatsoever. Among the many fine and rare items imported by these people archaeologists have discovered amber from as far away as the Baltic, Gold from Ireland and shells from the Mediterranean coast.

The Rituals of Death

Their society was tribal in nature, with a distinct social elite, and it appears that some form of priesthood was also involved in their social hierarchy. Although probably male dominated; as evinced by many of their burials, it is entirely possible, and in the light of similar world cultures even probable, that the blood line of the chieftains passed through the female line. In death the status of these chieftains was as marked as it had been in life. Their passing was marked with great ceremony and their graves, whether inhumations or cremations, were filled with the treasures that they had gathered to them in life.

One such inhumation, at Driffield in Yorkshire, gives us a clear view of the importance placed upon the rituals and ceremonies of death.

It is the body of a man, buried in a pit under a round barrow with a capstone covering it that took eight men and a windlass to remove. The grave's tall occupant was buried in the foetal position, his head to the east, facing south, and was originally wrapped in a woollen cloak or shroud. Attached to his wrist by four, gold covered, bronze pins was a polished grey slate archers wrist guard and at his side lay a fine bronze dagger with its wooden sheath. Where his neck lay were discovered two amber beads and behind his legs lay a decorated beaker. All the wealth of this world carried on into the next. Yet, no matter how we think we can understand such ceremonies, analyse the contents of the graves and study their bones, we can never fully understand the beliefs that they were based upon. The tall man, surrounded by his wealth of bronze and gold, also took one more item with him to the other world; the detached skull of a hawk had been carefully placed before him.

In East Anglia the Beaker people were particularly active and evidence of their occupation is more widely found than in many other regions of Britain. This may well have been an indication of the importance of the region, being fertile farming land and home of a large supply of high quality flint, or it may be the result of successive waves of settlers arriving from the continent. Their small round barrows, that supersede many of the earlier long barrows, still dot the landscape with over one and a half thousand being recorded in Norfolk alone. Of these there is also one very distinct group, over fifty in number, that all lie on the direct route of the Peddars Way.

It is to these people, the Beaker culture that arrived

from Europe in the third millennia before Christ, that we must look for the original builders of Seahenge. It is from their belief systems, coupled with the native traditions, that such a monument draws its meaning.

If it was not actually built by the Beaker people themselves then it was built by those who were directly influenced by them.

Yet, perhaps, I am again being too simplistic. The Beaker culture did adopt many of the religious sites of the native peoples, that much is certain, and it may well be that this is just such a case at Holme. Perhaps the actual timbers that make up the circle are simply a rebuilding by a later people upon a site that was already ancient and considered sacred by the native population. Is it possible that somewhere beneath the peat at Holme, or somewhere under the waves, lies evidence of even earlier ceremonial structures? One thing is certain; the people who first built the circle were most definitely not the last to make use of it. Activity in the surrounding area is believed to have continued for many centuries after the Beaker people had ceased to be identifiable as a separate cultural entity, as evinced by such artefacts as John Lorimer's Middle Bronze Age axe and middle and the late Bronze Age pottery sherds that have been discovered at the site.In the centuries that immediately followed the circles building technology advanced with slow but steady consistency. The use of copper for tools all but disappeared, bronze production improved, both in quality and quantity, and agriculture made enormous progress; leaving field markings that are still visible in selective places to this day. Burial customs changed; the people preferring to cremate their dead then bury the ashes in an inverted pottery vessel, rather than burying their bones. Yet, when these new peoples sought after the spiritual, when they practised their rituals of death and performed their ceremonies to ensure the safe passage of the departed to the afterlife, it was to the bleak and mysterious area surrounding Holme Dunes that they came.

Some Conclusions

The conclusions that can be drawn from the Seahenge excavation, and more importantly the debate that surrounded it, are numerous and perhaps more far reaching than anyone has yet realised. Like the environmental impact to the site at Holme itself the true consequences and damage have yet to be fully assessed. For archaeology in general, and more specifically its relationship with the public, it may be many years before the true extent of the damage becomes fully apparent. However, there are certain points that both the archaeologists, protesters and the public should bear in mind.

The first is simple and concerns archaeology itself. Excavation archaeology is, by its very nature, a destructive process. Every site that is excavated is, to a greater or lesser extent, destroyed. To gain knowledge and understanding of a site, be it a four thousand year old timber circle or an eighteenth century factory, it must first be taken apart, piece by piece and layer by layer, until nothing remains. The object of the exercise is, by carefully recording and interpreting the site as it is dissected, to learn as much as there is to know about the site in question and leave a full and accurate record for future generations. Once the evidence has been removed it is gone forever and only by leaving a full and accurate record, by following every guideline, can such a project be deemed worthwhile. If any of these aspects are overlooked, or compromised, then the excavation has been a failure. Taken to its furthest extreme, a badly run excavation is akin to academic vandalism.

However, archaeologists are, by and large, both well meaning and competent. All those that I have come into contact with show a deep feeling for, and understanding of, the past. They care deeply about the projects they undertake and approach them in a truly dedicated and professional manner and, if mistakes are sometimes made, then that is exactly what they are; mistakes. No archaeologist is going to become rich or famous doing what they do; the pay is poor, the conditions often extreme and, with a few exceptions, they are not going to become household names. The archaeologists of today are a far cry from the self seeking treasure hunters of the past. Despite being only a generation away from the likes of Howard Carter and Alexander Keiler their attitudes and approaches are a thousand miles removed. If they truly did not love what they do then they would not do it.

In the past half century archaeologists have been very much left to get on quietly with their jobs. Year on year funding, in real terms, has diminished and they have had to be satisfied with cutbacks, redundancies and developer funded excavations. Thousands of promising new sites have been recorded but, with no funds available, they have remained untouched. For the most part this has had virtually no effect on the public. Archaeological excavations have carried on where possible but, until a major, earth shattering discovery such as the Hoxne treasure or Seahenge has taken place, they have received little or no publicity. The archaeologists, with little media experience and submerged in the realms of academic study, have been content to let it continue in the same manner.

However, recent years have seen a sudden change to all that and archaeologists now find their profession to be fashionable and their excavations to be receiving lavish amounts of media attention. Suddenly history is back in fashion.

Programmes such as Channel 4's *Time Team* have educated the public about archaeological matters. No longer is archaeology and heritage the domain of the reclusive tweed-clad scholar and bespectacled historian. The general public has taken an interest and words such as 'geophysics' and 'dendrochronology' are no longer the exclusive domain of the experts. The man in the street now feels that he has a knowledge of the subject, understands how sites are excavated and is familiar with the methods used. However, this new found interest in the subject, and the subsequent raising of the profile of archaeology and archaeologists, is a double edged sword.

The new found popularity of such programs as *Time Team* has led to the public wanting a greater involvement in the way archaeology is carried out. The whole area of knowledge has been demystified and, as a result, the public now feel that they should have the right to discuss and debate archaeological issues. In the past the public, blinded by academic rhetoric and technical jargon, felt it best, if they considered the matters at all, to leave such issues to the experts. Now the barriers have come down, the experts have become media personalities and, as with all such celebrities, the actual value of what they are saying has decreased in the publics estimation. A four year excavation is now condensed into a half hour television program and while academic issues still guide such programmes one eye remains firmly fixed on the viewing figures. Familiarity, as they say, breeds contempt. . .

That is not to say that this process of bringing archaeology into the arena of public debate is an entirely bad thing. A better informed public is, given the right circumstances, likely to be more sympathetic and interested in the day to day work of archaeologists. Given the correct media 'spin' such attention can be turned to good use and can have long term positive effects on all aspects of archaeology. Unfortunately, we are still in a state of transition. While some archaeologists, and the powers that they answer to, are quite prepared to use the opportunities presented by this shift in public opinion to their own advantages, others are not. Many local archaeologists are still living in a pre-media age and

resent the publics intrusion into their cosy little academic world. They still believe that they know best and, although they very well might do, they are unwilling to open their minds to the possibility of public involvement and consultation. They see no reason to explain their actions at anything more than the most superficial level; they are, after all, the experts.

Preservation At Any Cost?

The most overriding question that still lingers after all the debate surrounding Seahenge has diminished is simple yet deep seated; and one that we must all think long and hard about. Should archaeological sites be preserved at all costs? It is a question that faces all those people, on whatever side, who care for Britain's heritage and is now a question that faces archaeologists at a world wide level. In North America archaeologists now find themselves severely limited when dealing with native American artefacts; to the extent that they are now having to hand back human remains that have been excavated for study purposes. Newly discovered sites are being denied them and no investigation may proceed without the full backing and support of the relevant peoples. The cry that they are only studying such remains to further historical knowledge no longer carries much weight with the native peoples whose sacred sites have been excavated and, in their opinion, desecrated.

The same problems now also face those who have been studying the remains of aboriginal Australians. Museums and universities world-wide are being forced to return any human remains that they possess for re-interment by the native people. Their reasoning is simple. What gives archaeologists and scholars the right to exhume their ancestors for academic research? By whose authority do they desecrate the holy places of the native peoples? If such questions are being raised by the native populations of such distant lands how long will it be before the same questions are asked by the native population of this island? Can archaeologists, in good conscience, continue to excavate spiritual sites and exhume the remains of our forebears in pursuit of knowledge? What price are we prepared to pay for a better understanding of the past?

The protesters who joined together at Holme to fight the proposed excavation of the timber circle have been portrayed by various sections of the media as the 'lunatic fringe', and yet this is far from being the case. It is true that they did contain a certain amount of Druids and others who are generally regarded as being far from the norm, yet these were the minority. The rest of the protesters were ordinary people; businessmen, local residents and tourists. Whether or not you believe their actions were correct it is impossible to mistake the depth of their feelings. Can we, in the future, allow such strongly held beliefs to be ignored? Is it right to simply excavate a site because the powers that be believe they know best? Mrs Justice Arden, sitting in the High Courts of Justice in London, believed that this was not something that could be ignored.

'Their actions (English Heritage) have been perceived as provocative by a number of people. To an extent the problems have been brought to a head by, for instance, removing the slice from the oak which is the central bole in the tree circle. It was a large piece of wood and is very visible. Secondly, there has been, I understand from Mr Needham, no local meeting, and thirdly, this is a religious place of worship for the druids and thus work done at the site has led to high feelings about the work being done. In those circumstances, to an extent, it seems to me that the claimant (English Heritage) must have brought this situation to a head by its own actions'.

The judge then went on to rule that not only should English Heritage supply a full account of their actions with regard to the chainsaw incident but, in future, they should take into account such points as the need for public consultation at a local level and the wishes of genuine religious groups such as the Council for British Druid Orders.

Despite the sympathetic nature of the statement made by Mrs Justice Arden it must be remembered that she did in fact rule in favour of English Heritage and it would be wrong to look upon it as anything other than a defeat for the protesters. A defeat that the protesters, had they been better prepared and more unified in their approach, could possibly have avoided.

A Lack Of Unity

In fact, the lack of a unified voice can easily be regarded as the largest single reason for their unsympathetic media profile. Although this lack of an overall spokesman was partly inevitable due to the diverse makeup of the actual protest group it did weigh heavily against them. Certain sections of the media found it all too easy to portray the protesters as the lunatic fringe and as a result popular support was not as forthcoming as it may well have been. In fact, the less vocal and more middle of the road supporters actually began to distance themselves from the movement as time went on. They felt that their own legitimate concerns had been 'hijacked' by the extremists and wanted nothing to do with them. How much this view was actually formed by the media itself is still open to debate.

Eventually it was quite possible, and relatively easy, for the protesters to be sidelined by the media

altogether. Their issues, however real, were pushed aside in favour of portraying them as a wholly negative campaign. They nearly all agreed that they did not want the circle excavated and removed; on that they were almost united, but they did not really seem to know, as a group, what should actually be done with the monument. Some favoured leaving it to the sea, others wanted it excavated and then returned to the area, while others even questioned, against most of the evidence, whether the sea would ever manage to erode the site at all. Their motives were brought into question. Some were portrayed as simply wanting to make money out of the monument, others as seeking self publicity and self aggrandisement while a third group, the group the media were only too happy to highlight, were seen as new age spiritualists and unreconstructed hippies.

This lack of a unified and positive purpose left the protesters onvery shaky ground and allowed the media to pick and choose to such an extent that, at the height of the campaign to stop the excavation, it appeared that the protest had more in common with the Twyford Down anti-road campaign than with a well reasoned local protest. Eventually, on the day of the mass occupation of the site by the protesters the whole story had become such a 'page five funny' that the national media hardly gave it a mention in passing; favouring rather the discovery in London of a Tudor banana.

To a certain extent this lack of unity and unified purpose still manages to dog the protesters. The site has been excavated and they have, to all intents and purposes, lost the battle. However, a large section of the original protest group still continue, against all the odds, to battle on. They want answers to their questions; answers that English Heritage, they claim, are unwilling to give. The conspiracy theorists amongst them are having a field day and once again the voices of reason, those that now simply want to know what will actually happen to the timber circle itself, are lost in the babble. The circle has once again been swamped; but this time rather than by the sea it has become swamped by the endless circular arguments.

However, it is all too easy to simply sympathise with the small group of protesters who decided to take on the might of English Heritage and the establishment. Many of them were, and to some extent still are, very badly informed as to what was actually proposed for the site and what actually took place. During the process of writing this slim volume I have been reliably informed by some protesters that the circle was removed by the authorities to stop the British people being able to understand and re-acquaint ourselves with our pre-Christian past. Others have told me, in no uncertain terms, that it was a scandal that *Time Team* were allowed to excavate the site in three days and that the devastating fire at Flag Fen was the direct result of a pagan curse. Some of the conspiracy theorists happily state that *Time Team* have actually bought the monument and that the excavation took place with unseemly and undue haste so that it could be used as a television Christmas special, for which the air time was already booked. When the media have such wonderful stories almost thrown at them it is hardly surprising that the less vocal, and more reasoned, protesters have found it difficult to make themselves heard.

Yet even these more reasoned protesters, those that want their questions answered by the authorities, must also face some harsh questions themselves. The circle was, and at the time of writing still is, privately owned and has not been given the status of a national monument. It was discovered on private land and the agreement to excavate was reached after discussions between the archaeologists, the landowner, the tenants and English Heritage. Why should anyone else, or any other small group of individuals, feel they have the right to interfere. To put it into perspective, if an important archaeological site was discovered in your kitchen would you expect the neighbours to be able to walk in and inspect it at leisure? Furthermore, would you expect the neighbours

to have a direct input into what actually happened to the discovery and where you should be allowed to position your fridge? The protesters must take a long hard look at their own motives. Those of them that truly are trying to save what they see as a unique piece of the local heritage must also bear in mind that they are not alone in their objectives. The battle to preserve threatened sites and monuments is ongoing and those organisations that they now find ranged against them would, in more normal circumstances, be considered their allies. People such as English Heritage and the Norfolk Archaeological Unit are only doing what they have been employed by us, the public, to do. They are attempting to understand and, in some cases, preserve our past. If they have fallen short of the expectations of a few, and the protesters really are in the minority, on this one site then perhaps those people should take a look at the massive task that has been set such organisations. Chronically under funded, bound up in red tape and faced with continual public pressure these organisations carry out an amazing amount of work; work that without which our view of the past would be infinitely poorer.

The Norfolk Archaeological Unit in particular faces an almost daily challenge of survival. Having recently been informed that it has to make a further annual saving of £20,000, despite the costs of the continued Seahenge debate and previous cut backs, the unit has been forced to make the county aerial photography officer, redundant. In a county such as Norfolk, where there are such relatively large areas of open land, aerial photography has proved to be an invaluable tool and has led to the identification of many dozens of previously unknown and unrecorded sites. In fact, in the field of aerial archaeology Norfolk always had the reputation of leading the way and its techniques have been emulated by many other county archaeological units, both here and abroad. However, the often spectacular work carried out by unit does not often make the headlines and a specialised officer is now deemed to be a luxury that Norfolk can no longer afford.

As to the Seahenge monument itself, it seems that the future of the circle is also likely to be largely determined by finances. With the cost of the initial excavation and preliminary investigations costing well over £70,000 it is probable that its future lies as much in the hands of the accountants as it does in the hands of the archaeologists. Any display and exhibition centre at Holme itself would cost many times this amount and it is unlikely that such funding will be forthcoming. The monuments owners are, according to English Heritage, 'keen to co-operate over a sustainable solution'. The latest twist in the tale came from English Heritage in March this year (2000). In a statement issued from their head office in London, English Heritage have now confirmed that the timbers will be returned to Norfolk for conservation. The work, which will be paid for by English Heritage and take place at the Rural Life Museum at Gressenhall, will take between three to five years to complete and will begin in September of this year. Only when the conservation work has been fully carried out will it be decided where the timbers will finally be put on display.

Why Seahenge?

I suppose, upon reflection, that the final question in the debate that has surrounded Seahenge must be the question that I began with. Why was it that this monument, a simple timber circle, caused such angry protest and depth of feeling to rise to the surface back in the summer of 1999? What was it about the project that caused such emotion? What made this excavation any different from the many hundreds of other excavations carried out in Britain in the previous decade? When Cath Saunt, the B.B.C journalist, ran the initial story about the 'Holme timber circle' back in late 1998 there was virtually no response from the public; no interest. What she had considered a good filler piece for local radio went out on several bulletins but was not immediately taken up by any other journalists. Then, six weeks later, the same story found itself hitting front pages and news broadcasts throughout the country. This time, however, it was called 'the Stonehenge of the sea', and later on simply Seahenge. It was this name, perhaps bringing to mind the ancient mysteries of Stonehenge, that captured the imagination. The 'Holme Timber Circle', as a title, has very little to offer the public in the way of mystery and imagination. It is a purely descriptive name. Seahenge, on the other hand, describes nothing. As a title it is incorrect, the circle being neither a henge nor built by the sea, but what it lacks in accuracy it more than makes up for in feeling and atmosphere. Few members of the public can tell you what the

definition of a henge actually is, but the image that come to mind is of the great brooding stones that stand on Salisbury Plain. It is this image, of powerful and ancient mystery, of other worldly majesty, that Seahenge carries with it.

The second factor that I believe helped to push Seahenge to the forefront of the public's imagination is that photograph. It appeared in national newspapers and on television for several days and even when the actual accompanying story was only a few paragraphs long the photograph was always prominently displayed. Taken by Mark Brennand of the Norfolk Archaeological Unit it is probably one of the most eye catching images to have emerged from the archaeological world in the previous decade. It is almost colourless; a stark black and white image that fades away into the distance. Sea meets sky and land meets sea. The black finger posts emerge through the rippling waters and surround the great dark mass of the central tree stump. It is a timeless image and, with no visible scale, it is impossible to gauge the true size of the monument. The circle could be ten feet across or, just as easily, a hundred. Had the archaeologists released any other image one wonders if the publics reaction would have been the same. If a person had been standing by the tree stump, or a Landrover been parked in the background, would the picture have held the same magical fascination. Would it have reached so deeply into peoples hearts and minds. I believe not. Like the name 'Seahenge', the photograph goes beyond the purely descriptive. It is an image that captures more than just light and dark and if one word had to be found to describe it that word would be, without a doubt, atmospheric. Today that scene is no longer visible; the circle is gone from the beach and will never be returned. That image can never again be created and the feelings that it evoked have ebbed like the tide. The atmosphere, however, remains.

The final word should, I believe, go to the protesters; the Druids and spiritualists who fought to save something they believed in. Whether their beliefs are correct is, I personally feel, almost irrelevant. Whatever your feelings about them, and the local protesters, there is no doubting the sincerity or the depth of their own feelings. They may not look at the world through quite the same eyes as the archaeologists, or even you and me, but perhaps that is no bad thing. Sometimes these debates have to take place, for everyone's benefit, and it often takes someone with a different perspective to even

recognise the questions that need answering. Government, at both a local and national level, must be accountable to the people, as should their appointed deputies and employees. Occasionally we may have to point this out to them.

I also feel that I should point out one other aspect of the whole debate and protest that surrounded the excavation; and that is the exemplary actions and attitude of the local police force. These days it is unusual to find such a confrontation where all those involved have nothing but praise for the police action, yet Seahenge was just such a case. The police were present at the site on a regular basis but took an attitude of non-confrontation throughout the whole process. The protesters tried to keep them informed of their intentions and this seems to have been appreciated by the officers involved. If the police, upon occasion, asked the protesters to leave the circle the offer was, just as politely, declined. No one I have interviewed has had anything but praise for their quiet, efficient and polite attitude – long may it continue.

On the subject of the police, a confession – when I began researching this book my sympathies lay almost entirely with the archaeologists. Having worked in the field of historical research for several years I thought that they probably knew best; a belief I still tentatively hold today. However, as the weeks passed I began to realise that the spiritualists and Druids, like many of the archaeologists, actually cared about the circle itself. To take it a stage further; although the archaeologists refer to the monument in academic terms and the Druids in spiritual terms, they are both obviously talking about the same structure; a

106

structure that is very dear to them all. To end I feel it appropriate to simply quote a letter written to me by Sam Jones, the founder of the Friends of Seahenge campaign.

'One last bit I would like to add to the questionnaire – throughout the Seahenge process, and still today, the issues, its meaning and purpose still touch at a very deep level. I have found some amazing strange people through this and some very close friends. Its like most of us kept our experiences and ways to ourselves and very rarely talked about them to anybody else, but the henge brought us together in a very spiritual, unusual way. I'm still not sure what should have been done. I have been to the very deep dark places of my own being over this and still wouldn't like to say it's definitely this or that. If it's right; that what comes from this is a greater respect for nature, a protection for wonderful natural sites, a greater atunement to feminine energy and wholeness with nature, then it has all been worth it.

Question: did I fight hard enough and should it have stayed in place? I don't really know. Have I the right to say? In the greater scheme of things does any of it really matter? – But I will just keep on questioning. . .'

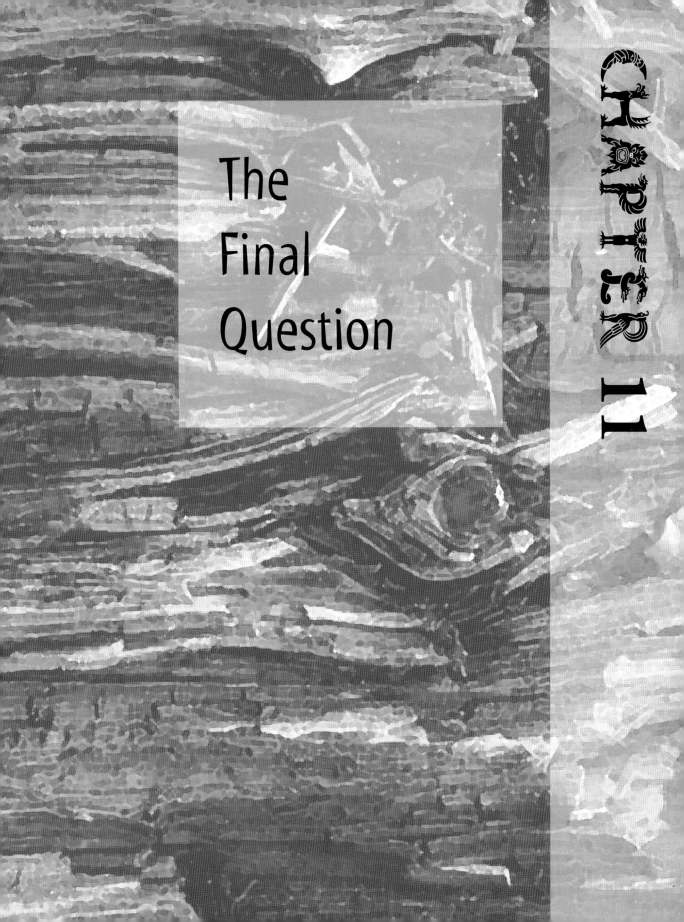

The Final Question

CHAPTER 11

From the very beginning of the main excavation, back in May 1998, the archaeological team working on the site always had at least one person available whose sole task was to answer any questions that the watching public may have had. Despite being out of the mud and water this job was not exactly the most sought after position and, according to those who were present, it was nearly two weeks into the dig before anyone actually asked about the archaeology present rather than the debate surrounding the excavation. With this in mind it seems fitting, perhaps, that the final question raised in this work should also concern itself with the debate surrounding the circle. When all else is said and done, was it right and proper to excavate and remove the timbers from Holme Dunes?

If, at the end of this publication you are hoping that I will give a definite answer one way or the other I am afraid you are going to be sadly disappointed. Having talked to most of those involved in the debate and

excavation, even if only 'off the record', I can see many sides to the argument and, to a certain extent, find all of them plausible. However, over the last few months four points have struck me concerning the circle and they are, I believe, worth repeating.

The first point is that the circle itself was being gradually destroyed, and at a much more alarming rate than many people would have you believe. Some of those from the Holme area believe that this circle has appeared, disappeared and re-appeared several times over the last century.

They claim that it was visible about fifty years ago, when a group of young boys discovered it while making their way along the beach to visit the Roman

fort at Brancaster, only to disappear again under the sands. Geoff Needham believes that this was the circle that he informed the archaeologists of back in the late 1970s and that it was once again buried by the sands until John Lorimer rediscovered it in the early summer of 1998.

However, if this is the case; if this really is Geoff Needham's circle, then, at the time, only the outer circle of posts were showing above the sand. The central stump was still well and truly hidden beneath the sand and peat and the interior of the circle presented a flat plain. When John Lorimer rediscovered the circle twenty years later it was the central stump that appeared first and the outer posts followed some weeks and months later. When excavation took place the tallest of the outer posts was at least eighteen inches lower than the central oak indicating that at least this much timber from each post had been eroded since the circles discovery

by Geoff Needham. Eighteen inches, at least, in twenty years.

My second point is that the discovery by Maisy Tailor of the infestation of the timbers by 'piddocks' was a dramatic pointer to the circles probable fate. These marine animals destroy timbers, whether they be Bronze Age circles or ships hulls, and they had already managed to bore their way up to eighteen inches into the main centre oak. Had they been allowed to continue unchecked, combined with the constant wetting and drying that the timbers receive from the tide on a regular basis, then the circle's life span as a recognisable monument would have been measurable in years rather than centuries.

The third point concerns the actual rate of coastal erosion occurring in the Holme area. Some people assure me that the problem is not a serious one and that the sands that wash away one year often wash back in a few years time, but, having carried out research of my own, I cannot share their beliefs. This may very well have been the case in years gone by but, as mankind continues to mess about with his environment without assessing the long term effects, the patterns of such erosion change. The coastal erosion pattern at Holme has undergone just such a change in the past fifty years. Construction of sea defences further along the coast have disrupted the natural patterns of tidal erosion and deposit and deep water sand and gravel deposits, that would normally replace material lost in the normal process of erosion have been dredged out for commercial purposes. This practice, banned by such far sighted maritime nations as the Dutch, leaves vast gaps on the seabed that the tide continuously attempts to refill with deposits from elsewhere; places such as the North Norfolk coast.

For those of you who would have more visible evidence of the changing pattern of coastal erosion I would suggest you simply compare the photographs of Holme beach today with those taken before the discovery of the circle. The peat deposits are now much smaller, many are gone altogether, and it looks likely that within my lifetime they will all be nothing more than a memory. Further evidence, and visually some of the most dramatic, is provided by aerial photographs. Just after the Second World War an aerial survey was carried out of most of Britain and if you compare those photographs with modern aerial shots of Holme you can easily see just how much of the foreshore has been eroded in a matter of fifty years.

My final point concerns the beach at Holme itself. The site is an internationally important nature reserve that is home to many rare bird colonies. Many of these birds rely upon the peat scarps as a feeding ground and the sudden influx of vast numbers of visitors did cause them harm. The full extent of this environmental damage has yet to be assessed. However, there are those who say that the peat, as I have already pointed out, will soon be gone and that the birds will then have to find new feeding grounds anyway. To them I reply that we must all, at some point or other, die; but does this mean that we should kill each other without thought simply because it is an inevitable outcome of life. The peat scarps are disappearing but that does not mean we should be the ones to hasten the process.

However, valid as all the above points may be was it right to remove the circle? I must admit that I am still undecided upon the matter. All of the points are good reasons to remove the monument but only if you believe that it was imperative that it be saved at all. Many people still believe that it should have been allowed to remain in place, record it, photograph it, even carry out trial excavations, but in the end let nature take its course. The circle was hidden from view by the peat, the sand and the sea for at least the last two thousand years, perhaps we should have let the cold waters of the North Sea finally take it away once and for all. The circle was after all a place of boundaries, a symbolic structure on the cusp between sea and land, life and death, the land of the living and the land of those who had gone before. Perhaps it would have been no bad thing if we had simply let it slip over the boundary for one last time.

Fire at
Flag Fen

n Thursday the 13 January 2000, as the Seahenge timbers lay soaking in their preservation tanks, fire broke out at Flag Fen. The blaze was quickly brought under control by the local fire brigade but not before considerable damage had been done.

Although the timbers from Holme were completely unharmed in the blaze, the centre, renowned for its pioneering work on early wooden structures, had lost both its Post Excavation Building and Educational Building. Although these buildings were an integral part of the site their loss was merely an inconvenience. The real tragedy of the event was that, along with many other valuable resources, the centre lost its entire documentary and photographic archive. The final blow came when it was realised that the centre's security copies of the archive, facsimiles normally stored in a separate building well away from the site of the fire, had been temporarily placed back with the originals while essential building work took place. These too had been consumed by the flames.

All those who have worked at the site over the past thirty years were devastated by the tragedy. The security copies of the archive had been found to be suffering from damp and had been moved from their normally secure location while emergency repairs were carried out. With space at Flag Fen at a premium, especially since the arrival of the Seahenge timbers, the only place that the archive could be stored was with the original copies. Among the records lost were site plans and photographs stretching back over three

114

decades and an appeal was quickly launched to try and replace them. It was hoped that anyone who had used the archive in the past, and may have made copies of any of the material, would come forward so that an attempt could be made to reconstruct the archive.

Although the site's managers were quick to stress that the timing of the fire was purely coincidental there were those who were more than happy to connect the disaster at Flag Fen with the arrival of the Seahenge timbers. In the days immediately following the fire rumours began to spread that a supposed Druid curse placed upon the timbers had been responsible, or that some of the Holme protesters, thwarted in their attempts to halt the excavation, had finally resorted to direct action. All such rumours, though damaging in themselves, proved entirely groundless.

The fire, devastating though it was, has not affected visitors to Flag Fen and the whole twenty acres of parkland, visitor centre and archaeological site are open as normal. Visitors, as well as being able to view the Seahenge timbers, will find a multitude of attractions at Flag Fen including a reconstructed Bronze Age round house and a replica Iron Age dwelling. For anyone interested in history, in particular Bronze Age and Iron Age Britain, the site is well worth a visit. Anyone who believes that they may have any documents or information that would be of use in the rebuilding of the archive should contact the site manager, Toby Fox, at Flag Fen on 01733 313414.